SO THAT OTHERS MAY LIVE

A FETHULLAH GÜLEN READER

SO THAT OTHERS MAY LIVE

A FETHULLAH GÜLEN READER

Edited and Translated by
Erkan M. Kurt

BLUE DOME

Published by Blue Dome Press
535 Fifth Avenue, Ste.601
New York, NY 10017-8019

www.bluedomepress.com

Library of Congress Cataloging-in-Publication Data Available

ISBN: 978-1-935295-20-4 (Paperback)
ISBN: 978-1-935295-29-7 (Hardcover)

Edited and Translated by Erkan M. Kurt

Printed by
IMAK Ofset, Turkey

Contents

Chapter Four
EDUCATION

Chapter Five
PEOPLE OF SERVICE

Chapter Six
ISLAM

PREFACE

The believer loves everyone and everything for God's sake. He
breathes with love at all times, forming an atmosphere of love around
himself. He rushes to stop the cries of mourning wherever he hears
them, and he applies balm to the afflictions of others. He turns tears
into laughter, helpless moans into praises to God, and storms of
fire into the breezes of divine grace. He suffers so that others may
not suffer. His tears flow so that others may not weep. If he does
not serve others, he considers himself worthless.

From "The Believer Standing before God"

This book is a selection of some of Fethullah Gülen's more
important essays. Gülen is one of Turkey's most renowned
religious and intellectual figures today and the spirit behind a
transnational civic movement dedicated to education, peace, and social
justice. He is an influential preacher, a scholar who combines tradition with modernity, a prolific writer, an opinion leader who inspires
millions, an educational activist, a lifelong advocate of peace, and recognized as one of the top public intellectuals of our time.[1] He has
published over sixty books, many of which have been translated into
more than forty languages, which are bestsellers in his native country.
Through his highly celebrated sermons and public speeches, Gülen
encourages a great number of people to pursue the ideals of service,
morality, virtue, justice, and peace. This *Hizmet* (Service) Movement,
or "Gülen Movement," as generally known in the West, is a loose net-
work of civic and humanitarian projects that include schools, tutoring
centers, universities, hospitals, aid and relief organizations, interfaith and
intercultural dialogue organizations, publishing houses, and media out-

---

[1] See *Fethullah Gülen: A Biographical Album* (Gülen Institute, 2010); *Foreign Policy*,
"Top 100 Public Intellectuals" (May 2008).

lets. Such initiatives today operate in about 150 countries, serving societies of different religious and cultural backgrounds.[2]

Fethullah Gülen was born in 1941 in Erzurum, Turkey. He attended religious schools, where he was trained in Islamic sciences; and the spiritual atmosphere of his family led him to become involved with Sufi circles. In his early youth, he was introduced to the work of Rumi, the great Sufi poet and philosopher, who would inspire him for the rest of his life. Said Nursi is another source of inspiration for him; his interpretations of religious sources in the context of modern science and philosophy left indelible traces in Gülen's mind. Gülen began preaching as a teenager, and at eighteen he was appointed an imam by the state department of religious affairs. From the beginning of his career, he adopted a very modest and yet socially active lifestyle. And through intensive personal study and reading, he improved his expertise in Islamic knowledge, specifically in Qur'anic commentary and the Prophetic tradition. He also became highly familiar with both Eastern and Western philosophy and literature, as well as writings in the natural and social sciences. Alongside his spiritual and intellectual development, Gülen took pains to be engaged with his community, initiating and contributing to various civic projects. His sermons, lectures, and speeches emphasized an ethos of altruism best summarized by his famous phrase *yaşatmak için yaşamak*: "living so that others may live." Rooted in the spiritual and humanist tradition of Islam, specifically Sufism, Gülen's message of service has been embraced by thousands of volunteers, who embody it in countless civic projects. Although Gülen (officially) ceased preaching in 1991, his advocacy of compassionate social service continues to this day.

Over the course of his career, Gülen has elaborated his vision of civic involvement primarily through his recorded speeches and essays. The former comprise published and privately-recorded tapes of his sermons, lectures, and public conversations. Gülen's essays have appeared in several Turkish periodicals from 1977 to 2010, and some of his

---

[2] For further reading, see Helen Rose Ebaugh, *The Gülen Movement: A Sociological Analysis of a Civic Movement Rooted in Moderate Islam* (Springer, 2010); Muhammed Çetin, *The Gülen Movement: Civic Service without Borders* (Blue Dome Press, 2010).

most important books are compilations of these writings. The *Çağ ve Nesil* (The Modern Age and the Contemporary Generation) book series, for instance, consists of nine books in which over 300 of Gülen's essays on religious, moral, social, historical, and cultural subjects are collected. This series is among the most important and representative collections of Gülen's work, and it was a major source of material for this reader. In another essay collection, entitled *Kalbin Zümrüt Tepeleri* (*Emerald Hills of the Heart*), Gülen treats Sufi concepts more specifically. Many of Gülen's books also include edited transcripts of his speeches or lecture notes; for example, his biography of Prophet Muhammad, a bestseller called *Sonsuz Nur* (*Muhammad: the Messenger of God*) was structured in this way.

This reader seeks to draw out the themes that are central to Gülen's many writings, through which he articulates his holistic moral project: a multidimensional ideal of prosperity that begins with individual virtue and extends throughout the whole of civilization. Gülen has dedicated his entire life, not only as a writer, but also as a preacher and activist, to the pursuit of this ideal. Viewing society and culture through the prism of "virtue," Gülen appears to fall squarely within the moralist tradition. At times, he writes like a moral philosopher in the vein of Farabi or Kant, concerning himself with the theoretical foundations of morality. But much more frequently, Gülen writes in the voice of a wise teacher, like Ghazali or Rumi, who demonstrates the boundless scope of moral life and hopes to motivate us toward the practice of virtue. Gülen's moral teaching tends to be more practical than theoretical, and he is constantly inspired by his own experience. Gülen treats ethical norms in great detail at both individual and societal levels, always grounding his references to tradition in the modern social context. He calls his audience to a total revival in virtue, to be "elevated" toward the ultimate goal of a lasting and shared happiness. This urgent "resurrection" requires that we recognize our privilege as humans and endeavor to live according to the enormous moral responsibility that accompanies it. If our modern society is to rise from its ashes, if a new renaissance is to come to our culture and civilization, we must be regenerated as individuals. For Gülen, such regeneration does not result in a futile longing for utopia but mobilizes us to work for the benefit of others.

So That Others May Live denotes this altruistic ideal. Throughout his writing, "service" refers not only to the lofty virtue of submission to God, but also to its necessary supplement: the work of serving all humanity for God's sake. Gülen argues that such service is the purpose of our lives as "God's vicegerents on earth." For Gülen, we live authentically before God when we dedicate ourselves to this moral project. If we wish to transform the earth into a paradise of virtue, we must work passionately toward this ideal. Living for God necessitates living for society. Service to God includes and requires the work of joy, peace, justice, and freedom. "To serve God is to be in harmony with existence and to be in unison with its members," writes Gülen. "It is an expression of comprehensive humility and submission to our responsibility as human beings." Therefore, Gülen repeatedly advises his readers to seek their individual ideals within the framework of social order, suggesting that social action is an indispensable dimension of piety. Often called *adanmışlık* or "devotedness," Gülen's conception of generous piety is not new to Islam. Rather, it is a return to the very *sunnah* (path) of all God's Prophets, particularly Prophet Muhammad, peace and blessings be upon him, and to the way of his sincere followers since the early generations of Islam.

Gülen's moral philosophy is optimistic. He accepts that only "seeds of goodness" can be found in the essence of humanity; evil is secondary and accidental, caused by our neglect of the good. Unless a man or woman totally betrays this "most beautiful" essence, all of us deserve love and respect regardless of our culture, religion, race, or nationality. For Gülen, we neglect the seeds of goodness when we are alienated from our Maker and from His moral purpose. The remedy for such alienation is the "love of God," which germinates and grows in the context of sincere faith and rich wisdom. As the love of God is the most abundant source of individual morality, it is also the most reliable warranty of a virtuous society. When we lack this love, the ideals of mercy, tolerance, peace, and happiness are beyond our reach. Gülen correlates the moral crises and social destructions of our time to the widespread spiritual famine that he finds characteristic of modernity. Nonetheless, Gülen does not completely discredit atheistic morality or consider it impossible, since the seeds of goodness are natural and universal. But he does insist that the love of God, another title for true metaphysics, uniquely enables us to attain, at both personal and social levels, a high moral ideal that embraces matter and spirit, body and soul, life and death, namely the human reality as a whole.

Although he takes Islamic faith and wisdom as his frame of reference, Gülen's call for a comprehensive morality has a universal character that can be reflected in all religious traditions. Gülen is not a universalist who expects different faiths to melt into one, nor is he a relativist who would approve of contradictory norms and not give absolute value to any single tradition. Instead, he represents an inclusive and all-embracing Islam that takes human commonalities seriously and praises virtue wherever it is found. If Gülen proclaims love, mercy, tolerance, and altruism, he does so not only because these values are truly Islamic, but because they are universally human. "We are first humans and then Muslims," he says, summarizing the humanistic dimensions of his theology.[3] The roots of this Islamic humanism reach back to the Prophet, peace and blessings be upon him, who, in an example that Gülen often cites, stood up while seated among his friends out of respect for the funeral procession of a Jew and explained his action with reference to an unconditional human dignity.[4] Perhaps the explanation for the scope of Gülen's influence lies here: His central argument is that Islam, so often associated with radicalism and now terrorism, is essentially and traditionally a space for humanist thinking. In this respect, his essays do not presuppose or require an Islamic worldview.

Gülen typically refers to *insan*, or "the human being," in his moral writing, and he uses this noun to designate three concentric groups.

---

[3] This aphorism relates to the "seeds of goodness" mentioned above: We are all created with the same spiritual essence; we are fellow humans prior to any determination. We are educated in or choose a particular religion only in the context of this fellowship.

[4] For this narrative, see *Sahih Muslim*, Janaiz, 78.

So That Others May Live

The first is the Turkish people, his compatriots—not as an ethnic group but as the mainstream cultural heirs of the Seljuk-Ottoman heritage. The second group extends to include his fellow Muslims, *ümmet-i Muhammed*, or the worldwide community of the Prophet. Gülen interchangeably refers to both these groups as "our people" and "our nation." As for the third, it includes the entire human family, the fellow servants of God, who share countless moral and religious values. Gülen's discourse thus addresses each of these three-dimensions simultaneously: the national, the religious, and the universally human. From this perspective, just as the terms "Islamic" and "human" reflect, confirm, and support each other, the distinctions of "local" and "global" communities intermingle and complement each other. Thus, even Gülen's address to his own country can resonate in diverse communities around the world. He seeks agreement with everyone, accepting them as they are so as to work with them toward the common good. There is a place for everyone in his culture of love and tolerance, the "sovereignty of the heart" that appears in his fervent writing, and he insists that to embrace all creation with mercy and sympathy is to proceed closer toward God. Gülen balances a deep concern for his own community, country, and religion with an equal passion for what lies beyond them. There is no duality, let alone discrepancy, in these two concerns; for Gülen, the spirit of a revelation demands "mercy to all." Just as a believer is a mirror to another believer, "a human is a mirror to another human."

Gülen's passion for the recovery and revival of Islamic culture, what he sometimes refers to as the restoration of Islamic civilization to its glorious past, does not come at the exclusion of, or isolation from, other traditions. In Gülen's vision, there is no absolute other; "our civilization" welcomes everyone, for it is the home of *insan*, the human being. Gülen's frequent references to Jesus as a paragon of tolerance are significant in this regard. Like the latter's famous words from the Gospel concerning the Sabbath, Gülen's message proclaims: "Islam is for man, not man for Islam." It is this humanist insight that inspires the projects of the *Hizmet* Movement, whose humanitarian aid campaigns reach all corners of the world and whose message of intercultural cooperation is being welcomed all across the globe. It should be noted at this point that Gülen's religious humanism allows him to preserve the values of Islam through practice, not proselytization. He is quite clear in this matter. He describes the ideal "new man" as one who "will enthusiastically practice his values everywhere." Such a practice is only possible within the ethos of a global society and free market in which different values are greeted with understanding and tolerance. In this great mix of cultures, Muslims should practice their faith in sincerity but acknowledge that their tradition is rooted in the universal values of mercy, love, and respect.

Gülen is a poet, and many of his essays reflect this temperament. I do not mean his frequent references to poems, which are surely quoted by heart from among the thousands of couplets in his memory, but the poetic flow of his sentences. Gülen writes with a pen directly connected to his heart, in an improvisational style that he made familiar in his sermons and speeches. He writes as if he were holding a mirror to his ever-moving soul, without presuming where his thought will conclude. And so when the time came to retranslate Gülen's essays for an English-speaking audience, I felt it appropriate to favor a literary translation to a literal one. I did my best to accurately adapt certain poetic phrasings, and where possible, make stylistic alterations that would preserve the extemporaneous, poetic quality of the original essays. Inwardness is characteristic of Gülen's style, and he rarely cites third parties in his writing. He assumes his readers to be familiar with a range of Islamic, artistic, and historical references; this edition has added footnotes to facilitate the interpretation of Gülen's flowing argument.

This reader contains forty essays, chosen to provide an introduction to Gülen's intellectual and spiritual adventure. Despite spanning about thirty years, Gülen's writing is quite consistent and does not demand a chronological reading. And, as my intention is first and foremost to provide a representative summary of Gülen's thought, I have chosen to organize each chapter by concept rather than chronology. Nonetheless, it is still helpful to consider the historical and political context in which certain essays were written. To this end, I have indicated the year of publication at the end of each article, and provided relevant historical information where necessary. I have given additional information and source details in the footnotes. I have also chosen to translate Gülen's characteristically inclusive *insan* (the human being) with the term "we" instead of "human" or "person" as has been translated in the past. Exceptions were made for passages in which Gülen's figurative language would have been confused by the grammatical shift. At times, it was necessary to preserve the third person nature of *insan*, but the tone of the passage required a word more personal than "human" or "person." We choose to use the masculine pronoun in these cases, as this made for the most fluent rendering of Gülen's often extemporaneous style. But conscientious readers should note that Turkish pronouns have no gender, and Gülen's message of tolerance is clearly directed equally toward both men and women.

The goal of this new translation is to preserve and present to a new audience the original intentions of the author. And so I am thankful to have been able, on several occasions, to receive special contributions to the text from Gülen himself: He approved the table of contents, offered clarification during the translation of many of the essays, and even selected the final title of the collection.

Thirty-four of the forty essays here were originally published as lead articles in *Sızıntı*, a popular monthly magazine in Turkey dedicated to religious and scientific thought. Four others originally appeared in *Yeni Ümit*, a semi-academic periodical for Islamic thought, and the remaining two in *Yağmur*, a magazine of literature, and *Zuhur*, a discontinued magazine of religious knowledge. Many of these articles have been translated to English and published in *The Fountain*, the English counterpart of *Sızıntı*. Several others appeared for the first time in *Toward a Global Civilization of Love and Tolerance* (The Light, 2004). Though this edition benefited from some of these earlier versions, each essay has been carefully retranslated in order to produce an original and consistent work.

In fact, I owe special thanks to the many people who have made this reader possible. First, I am especially grateful to Gülen himself for kindly honoring this project with the aforementioned contributions. I thank Osman Şimşek, one of the editors of Gülen's works, for his

help throughout this process, and I am unable to articulate my gratitude to Alex Dupree, my language and style editor, for his contributions. This volume would not be the same without his generous and
elegant work. I am further indebted to Y. Alp Aslandoğan, who came
up with the idea of a "Gülen reader" in the first place, and to Yusuf
Alan and Hakan Yeşilova, who helped me solve many technical problems. I thank Jim Harrington and Kemal Budak for reviewing the man-
uscript and suggesting many helpful points. Finally, I am so grateful
to the Gülen Institute at the University of Houston for funding the
project from the beginning. I hope this reader presents Gülen's ideas
and ideals clearly, so that they can be better known throughout the
English-speaking world.

E. M. Kurt

CHAPTER ONE

HUMANITY & CIVILIZATION

The Love of Humanity

L ove is like an elixir that gives us life. We are happy with love, and with love we make those around us happy. For humanity, love is life, and it is through love that we encounter each other. Love is the strongest bond that God has created among us; it is a chain that links all of humanity together. Without love, the world is nothing but a ruin. People have their kings, even bees and ants have their queens, and each takes the throne in a different way. But love does not fight for ascendancy, it is already enthroned. The tongue and lips, the eyes, and the ears then become love's fanfare, valuable when they proclaim it. But love is valuable for its own sake, and the heart is priceless when love has made its palace there. The flags and standards of love conquer castles without bloodshed, and even the greatest of kings will become love's humble servant.

We have been brought up in the presence of love's victory. Each new generation sees love on the throne and hears the drums that celebrate its reign. Our hearts pulse with excitement whenever we see the flag of love flying. We have become so intertwined with love that our lives depend on it. Our souls are dedicated to it. If we live, we live in love; if we die, we die in love. We feel love in our every breath. It is our warmth in the cold and our oasis in the heat. Love is made known in both our work and our rest. The drums of love accompany us in our struggle, and love's soft music turns peacetime into a festival.

If there is anything pure in this polluted world, it is love. Again, if there is any one of life's fleeting ornaments that preserves its beauty and charm without fading, it is love. In every nation, in every society, love is the most genuine and lasting thing. Even the most delicate melodies fall silent in contemplation whenever the voice of love, softer than any lullaby, is heard.

It is love that kindled God's will to be "known and seen" and led Him to create.[5] Without this love, there would be no moon or sun or stars. The universe is a poem that attests to God's love, and love is like the rhyme that gives order to the poetry of the earth. In the beauty of nature, we sense its presence. In our human relationships, we see the signs of its ascension. If there is a currency that always maintains its value among people, it is love. For love is valued for its own sake. It outweighs even the purest gold. Gold and silver can lose their worth, but nothing can diminish the value of love. Only the wildest hatred dares to struggle against it, and yet love is one thing that can disarm this hatred. There are many problems that worldly treasures cannot solve, many doors that cannot be opened except with the mystical key of love. For nothing can resist love, and nothing can compare to it. Even the most splendid and pompous barons of gold and silver cannot come close to matching its worth. For the day will come when their money runs out, their businesses close, and the fires in their furnaces die away. But love's candle has always been burning, and it will continue to give light to all hearts and souls.

Those who have humbly enrolled in the school of love and who have devoted their lives to its instruction are fortunate; there is no room in their vocabulary for hatred, wrath, or conspiracy. Even when their lives are in danger, they do not resort to enmity. They bow their heads only to love and do not acknowledge any other authority. And when they are inspired by love to act, hatred cowers in hiding, wrath goes mad with its own fury, and conspiracy brings trouble upon itself.

Love will dissolve even the most dangerous evil schemes. The Prophets extinguished the fires of hatred and anger kindled by the Pharaohs with the waters of love.[6] Empowered by love, the eminent friends of God tamed undisciplined and rebellious people, establishing community among them. The power of love overwhelms the spell

---

[5]   This refers to a sacred word, famous in the Sufi tradition, in which God says: "I was a hidden treasure; I loved to be known and thus created the universe to be known."

[6]   In Islamic faith, a Prophet (*nabi*) is a man chosen and prepared by God for the delivery of His message. Thus, all Prophets are morally perfect and cannot commit a grave sin.

of Harut and Marut and extinguishes the fires of Hell.[7] Therefore, a person armed with love needs no other weapon. Love is armor strong enough to stop any bullet or cannonball.

In order to care for our community, love humankind, and embrace all of creation with compassion, we must first know ourselves. In discovering our essence, we also discover our relationship with the Creator. And the more we know of our own inwardness and essence, the more we will appreciate the same inwardness in others. In this awareness, which knows that we all enjoy the same inward relationship to the Creator, we will see every creation in a different and unique way. Our appreciation and respect for each other is tied to our recognition of these inner relationships. It is as the noble Prophet said: "A believer is the mirror to another believer." We can even extend this wisdom to all people and say: "A human is a mirror to another human."

If we succeed in this, we will sense in our own depths the rich inwardness of others. And we will acknowledge that the riches hidden within those whom we love were bestowed by God. For every good and beautiful thing in the universe belongs ultimately to God. A soul that can sense these depths can speak in the language of the heart, saying like Rumi: Come, come and join us. We are the people of love devoted to God! Come in through the door of love and sit with us in our home. Through our hearts, let us speak one to another. Let us speak secretly, without ears and eyes. Let us laugh together without lips or sound, like the roses do. Like pure thoughts, let us meet without language. Since we are one, let us call each to other without words. Let us talk with our hands clasped together, as hands understand the language of the heart better. Let us keep silent, so our trembling hearts may speak.

This depth of feeling, in which the abundance of human affection is revealed, is an essential part of our tradition that we do not find in Greek, Roman, Latin or modern Western thought. In Islamic thought, every individual is a manifestation of the same essence; we are differ-

---

[7] Harut and Marut are two angels mentioned in the Qur'an, whom God sent to test the people of Babylon by performing magic (Qur'an, 2:102).

ent facets of the divinely bestowed reality. Indeed, all who gather into a community, whether united under one God or one land, resemble the "limbs of a body" of which the Prophet spoke. The hand does not compete with the foot, the tongue does not reproach the lips, the eye does not reprehend the ears, and the heart does not struggle against the mind. If we are complementary parts of the same body, why should this union be seen as discrepancy? Why should we disrupt the unity among us? It is in unity that we can make this world like a paradise, and through unity that we can attain Paradise. When will we remove from our souls the thoughts and feelings that alienate us from each other?

Humankind is a diversity of characters and temperaments, and there are as many ways to God as there are creatures to come to Him. Every person must understand in their own way, must walk across their own bridge, must ascend their own path. Each of us plays a different instrument and is enraptured by a different melody. This plurality is to be celebrated as we all seek to please God and make this world into paradise. The field is wide for running, and the end is open to all. Why then should there be any conflict? It would only gladden our enemies.

I would like to conclude with a couplet of a poet of our culture:

> *Woman and man, youth and old age, the bow and the arrow:*
> *each needs the other.*
> *Indeed, all parts of the world are in need of each other.*[8]

September 1999

---

[8] Basiri (d. 1534), Turkish-Ottoman poet.

The Inner Life of Humanity

Humanity is the essence of existence, its center and its distillation. We are the focal point of all creation, and all things living and non-living gather around us in concentric circles. The Creator has bound all creatures to humanity, and as we come to learn of our need for a foundation, the Creator will bind us to Himself. From this fortunate place, our heart is as vast as the universe, and we are able to speak the truth of things and proclaim the All-Powerful One. In humanity, existence finds its interpreter; we transfigure matter into meaning. We have been given a privileged understanding of the book of the universe; for we can relate each phenomenon to its Author. Grounded in this knowledge, our silence is contemplation, our speech is wisdom, and our last word is love.

We were created to preside over existence, and we are the ones who present the truths of nature to the Creator. We are the ones who sense the relationship between humanity, existence, and God, and who mold this relationship into wisdom. We are the ones who comprehend, in inwardness, the mysteries of our potential: that we can reflect the ocean in a drop of water, the sun in an atom, and ascend even higher than the angels. As we stand upon the earth, our heels become the crown of all creation. Humanity is the pride of the physical world, which boasts of us to the heavens. Creation is like an immense ocean, and we are its most precious pearl. The universe is a maze of gardens, spread out before us for our observation. History is a dazzling harmony of careful balances, and we are its witness. Life is illuminated in the light of our faith, and its beauty inspires in us feelings of Paradise.

Before humanity assumed authority over the earth, the angels proclaimed the glory of God throughout the heavens. But it was humanity that carried this proclamation into the heart of the physical world.

Thus this globe, so small in the midst of the vast universe, became heaven's equal, for it is here that we contemplate the metaphysical truths. For as long as faith has been our source of joy, Islam[9] our life, wisdom our sustenance and love our impetus, humanity has been the crown of creation, and the earth has been hungry for our light. God bestowed this position to us out of His special favor. Humanity has been honored as the nightingale of the world, the most precious rose in this garden of unsurpassed beauties, which is yet only a shadow of the Garden of Paradise.

It is no exaggeration to say that all creation was designed for us. This world was created to be a garden for us, its rarest rose, and the ocean of existence was created to house us, its most precious pearl. Indeed, the whole of existence depends upon humanity. It is for us, it is voiced by us, and it is at our command. So we must depend on the Creator who put this existence into our service. This interdependence reveals the purpose of all creation: to provide a context in which humanity can serve God.

The needs of humanity are great; they extend to eternity; for we were created for eternity, and we are the candidates of eternal life. Our wishes and demands are boundless and our expectations are infinite. Even if we were given the entire world, our appetite would not be satisfied; nor would our ambition be stilled. Humanity always longs, knowingly or not, for the infinite; we expect an eternal home. Anyone whose heart is receptive to truth will hope to see Paradise and its Supreme Creator, the most Beautiful of the beautiful.

Anyone who sees the truth manifest in the appearance of the world, who is aware of humanity's place within the universe, is already traveling toward eternity. That person will value himself and respect his Lord. But whoever is unaware of his place in existence cannot these things. Such a person cannot be said to know the Lord in a real sense, much less show Him respect. And this relationship of respect is the

---

9   In a general sense, "Islam" ("submission" to God) denotes the essence of all divine revelations in history. (*See* Qur'an 22:78)

truth of humanity. Without it we, who were made to be loftier than the angels, may sink to depths beneath the most miserable creatures.

"Faith" is the name for this relationship between God and an individual, and this faith can make every person into a "sultan," as Nursi puts it. But unbelief, or the lack of such a relationship, corrodes the human temperament and alienates us from our essence. Societies composed of such miserable individuals will suffer greatly from the vices of hatred, rage, lust, greed, deceit, hypocrisy, jealousy, deception, and conspiracy. Their people will be like wolves to each other, and those who succumb to such habits cannot be a society in the true sense of the term, they are simply an unthinking mob. Diogenes of Sinope warned against such mobs as he walked the daytime streets with a lamp, searching for human beings. Marcus Aurelius, the philosophical emperor of Rome, prepared himself every morning for the savage people that he would face that day, and he was happy in the evening if nobody had "bitten" him. Rabi'a al-Adawiyya, the great Sufi woman of the eighth century, was even harsher: She often saw the people around her in the form of foxes, wolves, and other predators. These wise persons do not condemn their peers by speaking in this way. They simply depict the misery of those in whom a lack of inwardness has led to an imbalance in human virtue. If we do not conform our appearance with the purpose of our creation, or check our character with regard to our appearance—if we do not strive to eliminate inconsistencies between these two levels—then we too will be as the wolves described above.

We often come across people whose visage is well-kept but whose inner life is in disarray. A writer compares them to buildings with two different façades: The front is clean and splendid, but the back is shabby and disgusting. We value the front side but detest the back. The same is true for many people. It would be a mistake to judge them according to a single aspect; we often glorify people whom we later discern to be wicked. In reality, those whom we judge as good may have many negative qualities, and those whom we judge as bad may have many positive qualities. We should strive to see them as they are, appreciating what is good in them and helping them to improve what is not.

As human beings, we are the outcome of our attributes, and we behave according to our dominant characteristics. Sometimes we are like Joseph, with his faces shining like the moon: We illuminate prisons and render them pathways to Heaven. Yet sometimes we are monsters who will eat our own brothers and sisters. Sometimes we are so angelic that even the spiritual beings admire us, yet sometimes we are so wicked that even the devils are embarrassed of us. Rumi says: "Sometimes angels envy our purity and courtesy, and sometimes devils tremble from our arrogance." These two poles of humanity may be distant, but they are interrelated.

The human being is heavenly at times, as glorious and immense as the sky, but we can also fall so low that it seems even snakes and scorpions would be preferable. Humanity is such a mixture that our merits often stand beside our disgraces. Even as we harbor countless beauties in our bosom, we are vulnerable to myriad evils. On the one hand, faith, wisdom, love, and spiritual pleasures are as close to us as our heart. Loving our fellows, embracing everyone, pursuing goodness, living for others, responding to misdeeds with favors, celebrating love, and fighting enmity... These are as warm to us as our own breath. But on the other hand, evil feelings such as greed, rage, hatred, lust, slander, mendacity, hypocrisy, conspiracy, selfishness, cowardice, and ambition are always waiting to ambush us. The merits of humanity more than qualify us to stand preeminent among creation, but we repeatedly succumb to our basest passions. Such missteps may seem to be the evidence of our freedom, but they actually reveal to us our miserable slavery. Humanity is free only insofar as we are victors in the inner struggle of virtue—designated the "greater struggle" in the language of Islam. For our potential goodness to flourish, and for us to attain the second nature that allows for relationship with God, humanity must attain the victory that is complete humility before God.

Whoever is incapable of the introspection that discerns both the vastness of our spirit and the hollowness of our nature will be unable to rise to each new day and will make no progress in their inner life. Despite their talk of progress, they will slide backwards. Such people cannot free themselves from the burden of their own egos, and they live and die as captives unaware of their fate. They are trapped in a pitiable enslavement to their corporeal forms. But they are still free to love and admire those who have nurtured their humanity, and these fortunate ones can show them compassion by helping them to escape this captivity. This attitude is an expression of love for those whom God has created to be noble and is the very expression of God's compassion. Surely, all humanity was created to be loved.

August 1999

Our Own Depths (I)

I am a lowly being, you say O man, but if you knew....[10]

T he self-control that comes from self-consciousness is one of
our most significant characteristics as human beings. But this,
ironically, is what too many of us neglect. How many people
can you point to who have made a habit of self-awareness? How many
people can you name who explore their inner depths, rediscovering
themselves every day? How many who recognize their frailties and
their strengths, their failures and their achievements? How many individuals examine their soul out of a true desire for self-knowledge, not
out of mere curiosity or humiliation?

Socrates often repeated the imperative inscribed at the Temple of
Apollo: "Know thyself." This ancient maxim, proclaimed in countless
schools of wisdom, acquired a divine dimension in the Sufi tradition:
"He who knows himself knows his Lord." I wonder how many people have lived up to this lofty formulation. I doubt the number is large.

Those who are not self-aware are not self-sufficient. Those who
have not discovered themselves are confined in narrow horizons and
cannot know anything but their immediate reality. Hence, their judgments are superficial and inconsistent. In the awe-inspiring mountains
of the earth, in rivers murmuring with the song of eternity, in the sky
filled with stars and mysteries more enchanting than music, the beauties of the other world glitter before our eyes. The truth shines from
behind the lace curtains of such appearances, and it is in our sight that
they find their true meaning. Apart from it, all existence would be nothing but chaos.

---

[10]   Mehmed Akif (d. 1936), Turkish poet, the author of the Turkish National Anthem.

Humanity has long attracted the attention of scientists, artists, and philosophers, for we hold so many contradictions together. We can be as sweet as honey, or as disgusting as foul slime. Sometimes we are attuned to eternity; sometimes our gaze is fixed on foolishness. Modesty and humility warm our souls, but our own pride and arrogance send shivers. We can be devious and treacherous, then transparent and trustworthy. We can be both selfish and selfless, aggressive and merciful, hypocritical and heartfelt. Insightful and perceptive, we can nevertheless be shortsighted and thoughtless.

But at all times, we are human. For these discrepancies do not arise from our essence. They do not relate to our instinct, nor are they proof of our endless malleability. On the contrary, this diversification testifies to the uniqueness of human nature: We are both spiritual and corporeal. Which we choose depends upon whether or not this nature is oriented toward eternity, whether or not we recognize our hidden potential, whether or not we give spiritual attention to our hearts, whether or not we give our willpower its due, whether or not we perceive the mysteries of consciousness, whether or not our emotions are directed toward transcendence, and whether or not we truly know the "mechanism" of our conscience.[11] Those who live their lives according to the axis of spirit, heart, and conscience, will always seek what is lofty, even if they stumble on the obstacles of their nature. As for those who remain in the prison of corporeality, with each moment they will sink more into an abyss, drifting away the ideals of humanity.

Those who consider the human being to be simply a "rational animal," or who define humanity in terms of subconscious or social determinations, have not put forward any profound idea concerning our genuine essence. Rather, they have made humanity into something ambiguous and complicated, almost unrecognizable. For some, we are rational animals. For others, we are slaves to the basic physical process-

---

[11] Gülen often uses the term "the mechanism of conscience" to refer to Nursi's description of conscience as consisting of some basic spiritual faculties. To Gülen, these spiritual faculties, as represented here, include: *zihn* (mind), *qalb* (heart), *irada* (will), and *hiss* (emotion, feeling, or sense).

es of digestion, circulation, and excretion. And for others, we live according solely to carnal pleasures, whose mind is a midden for the libido.

Although society, reason, and the subconscious are each important aspects of human life, we are not reducible to any one of these aspects. Our potential is such that, when destiny paves the way for our will, we are able to transcend everything in the world. History has demonstrated this to be the case. Each of us possesses an inner dynamism that can propel us beyond our own selves, even beyond all creation. And if we direct this mysterious potential toward its origin, we can transcend finitude and give meaning to our decaying mortality.

Today, we are able to harness thunderbolts, view subatomic particles, observe phenomenon millions of light years away. But we also suffer from a failure to understand the reality of our essence, futilely searching for it in corporeal spaces. All of today's savagery, selfishness, lawlessness, insatiable ambitions, indifference and self-indulgence stems from this mistake. Despite the all-encompassing genius of modern humanity, we are cursed because we have misinterpreted ourselves.

May 1993

Our Own Depths (II)

Realms are hidden in you, worlds compacted.[12]

I f the human being is a mere body, taken only in its corporeal dimension, then the progress of humanity is only a biological development, and we must resort to theories of evolution to explain it. Such rationale reduces humanity to the level of the animal, searches for him among the animals, and turns anthropology into a description of the barnyard.

If he assumes himself to be one of the animals, the individual will make material happiness into his ultimate goal. Pleasure, entertainment, and personal interest will become his ideals. And anything that facilitates these ends will be privileged above all else. In such a system of values, or rather a chaos of values, there can be no profound thinkers, resolute scholars, or diligent artists. Even if they could find a foothold, they would eventually be forced to cede to particular interests or else become dependent on the state. The recent history of our society exhibits this tendency all too well.

Nobody can deny that what afflicts people today is the materialism of modern civilization. We have grounded our scientific inquiries into life, consciousness, and human behavior on hypotheses darkened by naturalism. We have destroyed everything traditional in visual art and literature, we have pumped delusion and levity into everything, we have shaken social institutions from their foundations, turned governance and politics into an awful arena of mendacity and deception, and poisoned the family and the social body. Considering all of this, modern civilization seems to have cost humanity at least as much as it has offered.

From the perspective of "materialism," our civilization appears to be rooted in a gluttony that promotes greed and ambition over satis-

---

[12] Mehmed Akif (d. 1936).

faction and peace. More opportunity, more production, more credit, more profit, more comfort, more prosperity: It always promises more. As long as we misinterpret our true essence in this way, we will be captives to the very things that were created to serve us.

We live in a world where the profitable is typically preferred to the beautiful and the true. I think this is the essential reason why we have failed to overcome our present adversities. The "genius" of our age has exaggerated the value of science and technology and supposed religion, morality, virtue, and aesthetics to be unnecessary and useless. The shocks and sicknesses experienced in our nation and around the world will continue until the day we overcome this inversion of our values. I wish we had been awakened earlier to the true essence of humanity.

Spiritual reality is the truth of history and is embedded in it like a deposit of gold or silver. Once this spiritual reality is revealed, profit and entertainment will no longer have significant places in the hierarchy of human values. This spiritual essence is what distinguishes us from the rest of creation. All other creatures pursue their interests within the natural order. It is only human beings who pursue a meaning that transcends creation. Animals do not have religious sense or moral concern; they do not struggle for virtue or desire artistic creation. These are available only to the human heart, their sole devotee. The human being, born in religion and swaddled in morality, practices the pursuit of virtue and expresses himself through art. From the works of the most primitive tools to the marvels of modern expression, every voice and breath, color and line, form and pattern radiate from the prism of human nature.

Today, many of us wonder at the instinctive work of animals: the spider web, the bird's nest, the beehive, the beaver dam. But it is we ourselves who are deserving of amazement. The horizons of our genius extend to eternity. This is true despite the fact that today many of us are ignorant of the true values, the knowledge of which could elevate us to the summits of existence. Until then, God alone knows how many more fearsome tragedies, how many more floods of blood and tears, our materialistic vision will bring about.

June 1993

Our Responsibility

Humanity acts as God's "vicegerent on earth," favored among all creatures.[13] We are the essence of creation, the reflection of the Creator. He has placed us in this position and has given us our task: to discover the mysteries imbedded in the soul of the universe, to uncover the powers and potentials hidden in the bosom of the world, and to use everything to our purpose, embodying the divine attributes of Knowledge, Will, and Power. So as we engage with existence, fulfilling our role as God's representatives, we will encounter neither obstacles that cannot be surmounted nor impasses that cannot be resolved. We will walk comfortably through the corridor of events, developing what is in our nature without difficulty. As representatives of God, we will be able to realize our purpose without hindrance.

The achievements of the modern world testify to humanity's distinctive talents. Despite the destructiveness of these successes, they make it clear that we have not neglected our willpower. We have managed to reshape existence and change the very conditions of the world. This power proves that we are, whether we realize it or not, the confirmation of the divine word: "I am setting on the earth a vicegerent." At this proclamation, the angels worried that such authority would corrupt humankind, and we have proven their fears to be justified. But our goodness endures despite these passing evils; the virtuous ones of humanity have managed to spread goodness and beauty everywhere. Thus the seal of our vicegerency, entrusted to us by God, has not been totally neglected. A believer who has grasped the subtle wis-

---

[13] The term refers to the Qur'anic verse: *When your Lord told the angels: "I am setting on the earth a vicegerent," they said: "Will you set therein one who will cause disorder and corruption on it and shed blood, while we celebrate Your praise and proclaim Your holiness?" He said: "Surely I know what you do not know."* (2:30).

dom of creation understands that he or she has been sent to this world endowed with a distinct purpose, which demands a distinct responsibility. Vicegerency requires a certain morality, and our behavior must conform to this great task.

In the Qur'an, God states that humanity was created to know and serve Him.[14] This is the sole purpose of our privileged position among creation, our honored vicegerency. And the only appropriate response is gratitude, which guides us toward the proper use of our great gifts. In its broadest sense, to "serve God" is to be in harmony with existence and to be in unison with its members. Service allows us to move effortlessly through the mysterious hallways of the world. The human being is the intersection of the divine order in creation and the divine commandments of morality. Our inner life and outer existence are both from God, and it is service that holds the two in their proper relation. Without this balance, we are unable to respect our own moral values.

To maintain a good relationship with existence, we must act in accordance with its purpose. Whoever neglects this responsibility will run aground upon the universe in aimless idleness. He will transform the world, his home and palace, into an unlivable place. Many of us have already begun to tremble over the destruction of the natural and social order, fearing that such a hell is in the near future.

Only the One who prepared the universe for humanity can know the proper balance between the compulsory laws of nature and the moral laws of human will. The moral commandments come from such knowledge: They have been given in divine revelation. Conformity with these commandments gives us unique access to the mysteries of creation. This is the only way to live in harmony with nature and avoid clashing with the laws of existence. It is the only way we can truly be at home in the world. For alienation from the Creator and His moral commands leads to separation from His creation, and in this condition there can be no prosperity.

Our responsibility to represent the Creator must be actualized in our worship, our study, and our direct involvement with the natural

---

[14] Qur'an, 51:56.

world. In this respect, complete human beings allow faith to influence their every thought and feeling and let worship structure their social life. Only then do we find the balance in our families and communities that attests to the greatness of humanity. The complete human being develops the earth, preserves the harmony between nature and civilization, and puts the bounties of heaven and earth in the service of humanity with the Creator's blessing. In this way, we live up to vicegerency with which the Creator has entrusted us.

This task lies at the juncture of human effort and divine grace, and it is through service that we enter into this harmony. Service does not merely involve the performance of rituals, as many assume. It is an expression of a comprehensive humility and a submission to our responsibility as human beings. And service brings to light the true relationship between humanity, nature, and God. An attitude of service allows us to attain the consciousness of our commitment to God by liberating us from all other obligations. In service, our lives are directed toward God, and through Him, they touch everyone and everything. We relate everything to Him, and are constantly refreshed by our relations with Him, both theoretical and practical. One who carefully walks on the path of service never doubts his sole duty: to do justice to the responsibility that the Creator has bestowed on him. He seeks to live this temporal life to the fullest and to help others live it fully. He works to leave humanity's signature everywhere. He lives with a hope vast enough for the infinite and walks forward in the deep peace and delight that comes from being a child of eternity.

If we prioritize our responsibility in both natural and moral spheres, if we prize the spirit of service more than its results, then unexpected outcomes can neither disappoint us nor cause our enthusiasm to wane. Then we will serve God in others in the deep joy of worship, grateful that we have reached the apex of genuine faith. Then we will not despair, panic, or grow weary, but rear up like horses with renewed energy. Then like Rumi we will be able to say:

> *I have become a servant, become a servant, become a servant.*
> *I have bowed to You and doubled myself over.*

Slaves rejoice when they are freed;
Whereas I rejoice when I become Your servant.

We should measure the value of our actions not by their results, but by their truth, purity, and conformity to God's pleasure. In the same way, we should not let the concept of wage or reward limit our service, nor adulterate the divine work with worldly compensation. Devoted to infinity, we will attain the comfort of service to God and be liberated from the pressures of this world. As the servants of an authority that does not oppress or humiliate, we realize the freedom of our humanity.

If the human being is God's vicegerent on earth, he will work for God, initiate for God, love for God, create for God, intervene for God: He will represent God in all his actions. Therefore, he will neither be proud of his achievements nor in despair over his failures; he will neither boast of his abilities nor deny God's gifts to him. He will recognize that God has determined everything and assigned to him all of his works. With every achievement, he will turn toward the Lord to express his trust and refresh his confidence. He will remember the words of Akif:

Rely upon God, hold tight to effort, and submit to His providence.
This is the way if there is any; I know of no other.

With spiritual intensity, enthusiasm, and determination, he will see that all of his actions are service to God. So he will neither be arrogant in victory nor shattered in defeat. Whether he walks along a straight path or climbs the steepest slopes, he will continue his journey unfazed.

On the one hand, he must employ all of his imagination, all his mental and spiritual skill, in the service of his task. On the other, he must submit completely to God, faithfully receiving the consequences that are beyond his control. Yet he always pursues and always hopes. Here is the genuine believer and an exemplary devout! So many of them have left their footsteps on the path to Paradise, and so many are still walking toward the days that God has promised them.

April 1993

Woman from a Spiritual
Point of View

With regard to her inner faculties, a woman is a monument of compassion, and compassion first entered creation through her. As long as she remains true to her essence, she will always think of compassion, speak of compassion, act with compassion, and view those around her with compassion. And when she embraces everyone in compassion, her refinement and sincerity lead her to suffer with them. She passionately cares for all those around her: her parents, siblings, friends, relatives... and, when the time comes, her spouse and her children. When she shares in their delights, her countenance blooms with sweet smiles like a rose. When she sees others in grief and sorrow, she withers with them and groans in pain.

She wants to see beautiful things and be a part of a beautiful community. But there are times when she does not find what she seeks. Sometimes the wind blows harshly, shaking everything that is close to her heart; no matter where she goes, her heart cannot rest. Sometimes she is filled with anxiety and fights back tears. But at other times, she is surrounded by beauties that make her as joyful as a child, and she fills everyone around her with cheer.

A woman who has found her soul mate and who has quenched her thirst with her children is like a woman of Paradise, and the home that she builds is a "paradise" in its own right. Her children, who grow up savoring compassion in the shade of such a garden, will become like the heavenly beings. Indeed, those who have been raised in such a home will have already experienced the joy of Heaven, and their smiles will inspire joy in all those around them.

Even though the members of such a home are separate individuals, the soul that governs them is one. And this soul, emanating from the woman and encompassing the entire home, makes its presence felt like a guiding force. A blessed woman who has not blocked the way of her spirit nor darkened the horizon of her heart is like a pole star: She holds her position as the family turns around her. The others take their places around her and express devotion to her in their every movement. Their time at the home is limited and relative, but the woman, even when she works at another job, always provides the home with its heart. She offers her family the food of compassion and love that nourish their souls.

A woman whose thoughts and feelings are oriented completely toward eternity can inspire in a way that no master or teacher can. She adorns our hearts with calligraphies of the most splendid meaning that cannot be erased. She provides us with the spiritual depth that will ensure our victory in later life. In the presence of such a perfect woman, we feel the mercy and poetry of the other world pouring into our souls, and we breathe deeply in its joy.

A woman, particularly as a mother, is as immense as the heavens, and her feelings and thoughts are as numerous as the stars in the sky. She is always in harmony with her situation, at peace with her joys and sorrows, and closed to hatred and enmity. In her constant efforts to revive and restore, she is the purest representative of the divine grace on earth. The fortunate woman, who has opened the doors of her heart to eternity, stands brilliantly beyond imagination, perfect in body and spirit. Compared to this eternal dignity, even our highest praise to her is like a flickering candle.

We consider woman to be the most significant among all of the phenomena of creation, the most fruitful and wonderful element of all humanity, and an impeccable picture of the beauties of Paradise. She bears new life, and she nurtures our community. Prior to her creation, Adam was alone in a nature devoid of spirit, and humankind was doomed to extinction. The home was merely a den, no different than a hollow tree, and man was confined to the mute limits of his own lifetime. But with her, a second voice enlivened existence, and creation was made complete. The lone human became a species; only then could humanity assume its proper place in the universe.

Although women have different physiological and psychological characteristics than men, this does not denote either superiority or inferiority. We could compare this difference to the difference between nitrogen and oxygen in the air: Both elements serve a unique function, and both need each other to the same degree. It is meaningless to say, "Nitrogen is more valuable" or "Oxygen is more beneficial"; it is equally meaningless to compare the relative value of women and men. Woman and man share the same divine creation and mission in the world; they are like two faces of a single reality.

> *Woman and man, youth and old age, the bow and the arrow:*
> *each needs the other.*
> *Indeed, all parts of the world are in need of each other.*[15]

Sadly, the value of woman has gone unrecognized at times in human history. In some cultures, women were deprived of basic human rights, and considered more hazardous than poison. They were depicted as purely emotional creatures from whom men should flee. In other places, women were kept at home as maids, under the authority of their husband, or even sold by their fathers as slaves. Women have been disparaged as a burden or a shame to their families. In some communities, they were not even named, but rather referred to by number. In others, women were simply considered the means for reproduction. Even the giants of philosophy have contributed to this embarrassing tradition, condemning women as the gatekeepers of hell, the underdeveloped portion of humanity, obstacles to the greatness of men, or even mistakes of creation.

But Islam, with its message of eternity, restored the rights of women, offering them strong ethical and legal protection. The Qur'an elevates woman to her true place among creation, teaching clearly that women have rights just as men do. In his farewell sermon, the Prophet emphatically advised that men should treat women with kindness and respect and fear God concerning this. It is fair to say that Islamic precepts about women's rights were historically unprecedented, freeing her from the captivity she had experienced. On this

---

[15] Basiri (d. 1534).

fact, many writers, Muslim and non-Muslim alike, agree. Maurice Gaudefroy-Demombynes, author of *Muslim Institutions*, claims that the Qur'an pioneered principles for the protection of women that are more convenient than many modern European laws. Likewise, the British orientalist Stanley Lane-Poole argues that Islam is unique in respect to its historic revolution in women's rights.

God created woman to be a partner with man. Adam could not be without Eve, and Eve could not be without Adam. This first couple became the first representative of God: They mirrored the attributes of their Creator and became the interpreters of the rest of the creation. They were like two bodies with a single soul, representing two different faces of a single truth. In time, crude understanding and rude thinking forgot this unity, and the harmony of the family and the social order were disrupted. As the great Sufi poet Ibn Farid put it, the beauty of woman and man was the original glimmer of the beauty of the Creator, the Most Beautiful. These two marvels of creation stood hand in hand, shoulder to shoulder. And as each accepted the other in their respective places, they became even more beautiful. But throughout history, we have misinterpreted our roles and corroded our relationship. In particular, the beauty of woman—that multidimensional mirror of the spiritual beauty that transcends bodily adornment—has been dimmed by our preoccupation with her physical nature, thus have we narrowed the scope of her greatness.

As long as women are conscious of their inner depths and remain within the bounds of their nature, they will reflect the essential beauties of existence. Those who enjoy this reflection will free themselves from the darkness of physicality, ascend to the horizons of divine beauty, and recite in their hearts:

> *The sun of the beauty of pretty faces sets in the end;*
> *I am the lover of the Everlasting Beauty, "I do not love what sets."*[16]

April 2000

---

[16] A phrase from a Qur'anic verse (6:76) about Prophet Abraham rejecting and condemning the worship of the sun and stars.

The Society of Peace

Throughout our history, peace has been like the distant beloved whom we mention at every opportunity, but with whom we never reunite. Instead, we languish in the world as in a barroom full of worries and complaints. Each new disturbance inspires in us nostalgia for their lost peace. It seems as if peace and its absence are circling each other across the worried face of history, as night circles day. Peace has never escaped this circular relation; it has always, in some sense, been defined according to its absence. How could it be otherwise? This world is not a place for absolute peace or for its absolute absence, but only a passageway to such permanence in the Hereafter.

Throughout history, only those individuals who have given their willpower its due, who have realized their divinely granted potential, attain peace in their heart and conscience. But those who could not comprehended the mystery of existence, who developed their potential in the name of evil, and who became captives of their base desires: they have been left to an absolute absence of peace.

For the believers on the path of truth, this absolute absence of peace is out of question. They will receive the glad tidings of hope in the face of every disturbance, so they can smile in the face of whatever comes their way. In this respect, faith and hope constitute the first condition of peace. As those without an exalted conscience and without a paradise within cannot attain true peace, those who await the future with hope, and who found a paradise in their heart through the expectancy of the joyful life to come, cannot be deprived of it.

We should direct all of our efforts toward helping people build a society of peace, on both a national and global scale. This society will be purified of all contemptible feelings and directed toward lofty ideals. Its individuals will rest in the serenity of their conscience, families will shine with trust and happiness, and communities will pledge agreement. Peace begins in the individual, resonates in the family, and from there pervades all parts of the society. Thus we must keep in mind that, if our aim is to attain peace through goodness and beauty, hope and security, our work must begin with the individual; for it is the individual who will shape the family and contribute to the life of society. From this perspective, a society made up of individuals immersed in error cannot promise any hope, happiness, or peace. These values accompany those who, with intellectual and spiritual depth, have comprehended the mysteries of the self. Only after we are secure in ourselves can we become good family members and fully-realized citizens.

The homes constituted by such noble individuals resemble the corners of Paradise. In these blissful hearths, the relationship between family members does not begin with birth or end with death. In the unending play of family life, new festivities are constantly being prepared for us in the realms beyond. Time cannot erode the sound structure of the family, and time cannot do damage to the compassion that holds its members tightly together. Such a sound home will continue forever, and its harmony and strength will be the foundations of a promising nation. It is the virtue and purity of the family that upholds the nation. And if the nation loses touch with this foundation, it loses its vitality. A people who do not depend on the bonds of family lose their identity. Surely, the values of love, respect, cooperation and solidarity that define the family are also needed in the life of the nation. Only then will the nation be able to determine history and serve the international balance of global peace and justice.

In a society of peace, it is the harmony among families, the unity of manners, and the sense of altruism in individual hearts that binds people to one another. The sufferings and pleasures of individuals are felt by the entire community. The people respect and support the state, just as the state serves people. The statesman seeks the joy and pleasure of his constituency. The boss stands by the worker and never overburdens him. He treats his workers like family, shares with them, and cares about their needs and rights. Likewise, the workers stand by their work and their employer. Free from hostility, they present their most exemplary effort and hope to be appreciated by God both now and in the Hereafter. The educational institutions are designed to instill a sense of virtue in students, open the doors of love and kindness in their hearts, and teach compassion for all of humanity to new generations. Teachers guard their students against ruthless ambition, base desires, rudeness, and shame, and students learn to respect the concepts sacred to society. Finally, the judiciary rules in justice, pursuing the wrongdoer and aggressor while guarding the innocent and oppressed.

Whoever works for this ideal will consider any possibilities that could allow for its realization. Only God knows how long we must continue this endeavor toward peace.

August 1979

The Ideal Society

An ideal society is composed of ideal individuals, so we should seek to define the ideal society according to the traits of the ideal person. As for the many who live in error, these crowds are not receptive to goodness and beauty.

The ideal person, or the "perfect human" to use traditional terms, is a person of insight and comprehension. He knows that, both physically and spiritually, he was "created in the best form."[17] He is aware of humanity's unique position as the candidate of spiritual ascension: *"We offered the Trust to the heavens, the earth, and the mountains, yet they refused to undertake it and were afraid of it; humankind undertook it."*[18] And he is capable of utilizing this divine gift. Indeed, we are on our way to perfection when we live according to the divine guidance. When we exercise our willpower over the gifts God has given us, when we cultivate them like a fruitful harvest, they are immortalized.

The ideal person faces up to the challenging questions concerning life, death, adversity, his place in the universe, and his relationship with God. Out of the answers to such inquiries, he builds a luminous tower of wisdom and, ascending its zenith, he comprehends the ultimate reality. Then he returns to the ultimate origin of the spirit in admiration, confidence, and satisfaction.

A soul that has achieved such heights will not be spoiled by further blessings nor shaken by loss. He receives felicity and adversity in his personal life with indifference. Others may feel arrogant or desperate, but he remembers only his responsibility, from which he draws strength. Therefore, he succeeds even in times of loss. Even when he faces formidable adversity, it is as if he strolls through this turbulence with assur-

---

[17] Qur'an, 95:4.
[18] Qur'an, 33:72.

ance. Even in the most difficult moments, he feels the breezes of peace that originate in the realms beyond, and praises God in total humility.

Thanks to his faith in the authority of God, the ideal human possesses the utmost confidence. Pure belief takes root in the depths of his heart, and his thoughts are free to explore the unfathomable dimensions of the spiritual world. With ears attuned to such depths, he hears the heavenly voice: *"Have no fear or grief, but rejoice in the good news of Paradise, which you have been promised."*[19] Or, *"Peace be upon you. Enter the Garden as a reward for what you have done."*[20] And the comfort he takes here will be his loftiest delight.

The ideal human sincerely believes in the realms beyond and structures his life accordingly. He is always far from guilt, crime, injustice, and disgrace. His desires do not set him adrift, for he struggles against them. His gaze is focused on the beauties of God, his mind is fixed upon eternity, and his heart is like a bright and colorful garden, open to angels and spirits. While there are many who pursue their corporeal pleasures but do not attain peace and satisfaction, the ideal person is a man of spirit. He will achieve peace and satisfaction as he serves humanity in knowledge and wisdom. The ideal human is determined to eliminate cruelty and injustice from the earth. He courageously responds to his oppressor with love, forgives with humility, offers tolerance toward the inappreciative, and when necessary, heroically defends his community against aggressors.

This man of spirit, who knows that everything but God is mortal and transient, does not surrender to anything and is not deceived by anything. He uses all that he has to help revive religious and moral virtues in society. He contemplates the world around him and works for the happiness of those who will come after him. Then he will pass away without regret, saying: "Long live the future generations!"

The ideal man always pursues God's pleasure in the truth. Neither material nor spiritual rewards can distract him, for he considers service to be the greatest value. By this criterion, he recognizes all of

---

[19] Qur'an, 41:30.
[20] Qur'an, 16:32.

God's servants to be nobler than him and gives them his utmost respect. He extinguishes the fires of confrontation in his bosom, so that no dissension would come from him. In this way, he overwhelms the misdeeds of others with kindness. He transforms the violence of lightning and thunder into illumination that enables others to see. His enlightened attitude can turn even Nimrod's fires into something "cool and safe" that brings peace to ill-tempered souls.[21]

We are working toward this ideal society, but many of us have not yet attained such quality of character. We do not overcome misdeeds with kindness; we respond to animosity in the same way as all others. We often mistake our desires and ambitions for our own thoughts. We thus adulterate our service with personal emotions, and so we lose even in our service.

June 1990

---

[21] Nimrod was the cruel king who attempted to kill Prophet Abraham by throwing him into a fire, which was transformed by God's command into a "cool and safe" place. (*See* Qur'an, 21:69)

The Concept of Civilization

The term "civilization" can refer to any community—a village, a city, or a nation—that is bound together by human virtues. Humanity has lived in civilizations of one kind or another since the beginning of history, but we are only civilized when we manifest ourselves as truly civil. Some identify civilization with industry, technology, or urban development. But these can only be the instruments of a prosperous life insofar as they are accompanied by human virtue; they should not themselves be mistaken for the essential elements of civilization.

Modernization can change the appearance of life, but it does not necessarily civilize people. True civilization is marked by the growth of human capabilities, and the civilized person is the one who flourishes spiritually and intellectually in the service of society. Therefore, civilization is first and foremost a spiritual and intellectual reality; it is not found in riches, luxury, or palaces. It cannot be found in production and consumption governed by the demands of corporeal pleasure. Rather, civilization is to be found in the ethical sphere.

Throughout our history, there have been many who sought civilization in material prosperity and have driven the masses toward modernization. This delusion has wasted our time and left wasted lives behind. Should we not instead seek the civilization of the soul that is spiritual perfection and self-renewal? Civilization is not like a garment that can be purchased and put on. We must envision it for ourselves and carefully prepare for it, taking into account all that is required for civilized generations to flourish.

In this regard, civilization is essentially different from mere modernization. In the former, people are intellectually and spiritually renewed; in the latter, it is only the facilities of life that are different. Nonetheless, whole generations have been duped by this confusion.

They have been misled by confusion of concepts and by a distorted vision of the true value of faith, philosophy, morality, and culture. This is how nations degenerate. As they enjoy modern means and technical facilities, their elite classes begin judging who is civilized and who is not, thus committing the gravest sin against culture, which history will never forgive. Just as civilization is not identical to modernization, education is thoroughly different from enlightenment. There are many enlightened people without formal degrees, just as there are many well-educated but narrow-minded people with little sense of civility.

Such confusion in our concepts can lead us far astray. There seem to be many places in the modern world where black is called white, where tyranny wears the crown of justice while true justice is oppressed; dark souls are introduced as disciples of light, while the truly enlightened are considered to be ignorant: Such confusion is too often celebrated in the name of progress.

An enlightened society, freed from this confusion depends upon the existence of a genuinely enlightened people. Society is illuminated primarily by them—not those with degrees in natural and mathematical sciences. Aware of the needs of their time, these enlightened ones remain true to their heart and spirit, their mind and will. A perennial source of light shines inside them; they synthesize their inspiration with their thoughts and constantly share this light with the whole of society. Civilization is the result of their work, for they are shaped by true thought and belief; every new civilization is born out of their love and faith.

There can be no hope for a civilization in which there is no such love or faith. If a society is under despotic pressures, even the most incredible scientific breakthroughs cannot herald the coming of true civilization. In this context, it would be impossible to sustain any technological advancement. If a community is deprived of faith, love, and a sense of responsibility, no amount of science can establish a civilization there. Even if all institutions are renewed, the standard of living improved, and all apparel is modernized, civilization cannot be manufactured through technological change alone; it is an intellectual and spiritual endeavor. Otherwise, we could "civilize" an individual in a few short months and an entire society in a matter of years.

But alas! Our failure to advance in wisdom, despite our clear and rapid modernization, provides the most tragic evidence that civilization has nothing to do with the adoption of modern means and institutions. The intelligentsia of our nation, inspired by their colonial mentors, has long advocated for such a delusion, misleading the masses by presenting the developments of modern technology as if they were the promises of civilization. Our religion, language, and philosophy have been ruined, and thus the pathway to true civilization has been blocked. Whatever their intentions, the result of this mistake has been widespread destruction.

Fortunately, our people have recently sought to gather around traditional human virtues and establish civilization in its true sense, and this has ruined the plans of the colonial powers. It will be the duty of new generations to devote themselves to such an ideal in determination and faith.

August 1985

The Nature We Have Destroyed

Nature is an exhibition of wonders, a book that we ponder in admiration. It appears before us every morning arrayed in a new, dazzling dress. Nature is a source of spirit and life, and it enraptures us.

Once upon a time, this display was dazzling beyond imagination. Nature was like a magnificent vessel sailing toward the country of love, or a chandelier with a thousand lights illuminating the realms beyond. With emerald hills and cool valleys, teeming forests full of animals, it was the shoreline of the other world. Its gardens and orchards were reminiscent of Paradise, with singing birds and laughing insects, with rain that poured like a divine blessing from the sky, as the praise of pure hearts ascended to the heavens in gratitude. In those days, nature was radiant with the beauties of divine power. Humanity lived so intimately with nature that they tasted the glory of the realms beyond and trembled in awe.

Just as the elegance and grace of a palace might inspire us to contemplate things beyond the palace itself, nature inspires in us the intuition of the ultimate Source of beauty, who designs the world and brings it into existence, yet still remains beyond our perception.

The architecture of nature brings us to the gate of the realms beyond. The mountains rest their heads on the skirts of the heavens, desiring to know them. Like the bees that fly from flower to flower, our imagination follows these natural beauties out to their furthest horizon. And once we arrive there, we believe that a new journey will lead into the infinity beyond the heavens. Then we begin to hear in the depths of our soul melodies from the realms beyond. Those who can continue in such realms will encounter the true Beloved, whom they have been longing for, and they will not want their journey to cease.

For those who have resolved to make this journey, nature—its exhilarating vistas, colorful slopes, impressive mountains, charming gardens, awe-inspiring woods, murmuring brooks and rivers—is a realm of pleasure, joy, peace, and imagination. Every corner of this display presents a different magnificence, a different poetry, a different charm. It is as if all the beauties of nature were in competition with each other, and we can only say: "It could not be more glorious." Those who are awakened to these beauties begin to experience existence more deeply; they begin to hear melodies everywhere. In the intoxicated gaze of these hearts, the trees whirl like dervishes, chanting the Name of their Creator, and the flowers proclaim His glory in their own language. Indeed, the delightful colors of the lilies, violets, lilacs, roses, carnations, jasmines, camellias, orchids, and magnolias whisper to us many secrets of the beauty of God. In the presence of such natural beauty, time is enriched; it is as if we experience all of the beauties of the time of our ancestors.

Nature is full of special places so charming that, when we are there, we feel near to the ultimate haven of beauties. We begin to see how our world is intertwined with the other, and we observe Paradise on the hills of this world. Our rivers murmur with the sound of Paradise. Trees sway in the breeze as if in the gardens of Paradise. In the beauties of nature, we feel and observe eternal beauties. Then we realize that life is too short to experience such pleasures, and we grow excited with an intense desire for eternity. Finally, we turn toward the All-Powerful One who can uniquely realize this vital desire.

What a pity that this magnificent book of nature, this charming display of beauty, presented by the All-Merciful One for our contemplation, is treated like a heap of junk. Nature is ruined by pollution and desertification. Smoke suffocates the air, that magnificent dominion of the divine command. The waters, those springs of life and grace, are made turbulent by perilous floods or, polluted, flow like pitch. And the earth, that storehouse of divine bounty and benevolence, is like an infertile wilderness, a ruin without balance.

Like much of what has been entrusted to us, nature suffers under our mistreatment. We have misused the plains and valleys; we have betrayed the rivers and seas; we have polluted the air and water; we have taken the gardens and forests for granted. Or rather, we have betrayed ourselves by turning this paradise of natural beauty into a hell. If we fail to restore what our hands have destroyed, nature will collapse like a heap of wreckage in a series of catastrophes.

January 1990

Toward the Sovereignty of the Heart

In our recent history, humanity has drifted from suffering to suffering. We have walked through pits of death, and our search for deliverance has only led us to new calamities. Around the world, established governments have cowed to the greed and ambition of individuals. Today, it is the untouchable elites, big companies, and powerful mafias that control our society. Human virtues are neglected, and people are preoccupied with a "standard of living" that exalts riches, property, and comfort. Like an arrogant gladiator raising his hands in victory, material wealth stomps out the values of virtue, knowledge, contemplation, and courage on which we once relied. But wealth has no value outside of this moral context. If we pursue it for itself, it becomes the cause of brutality. Yet wisdom and morality, the true core of society, have been despised as fantasy and foolishness.

If a society is structured according to corporeal demands, if its people live their life in thrall to pleasure and enjoyment, thinking of nothing but their own prosperity, then those who are aimless, deceitful, sordid, careless, ignorant, and shortsighted will prosper at the expense of those who are diligent, the industrious, and the well-tempered. To exclude the considerations of morality and virtue from society is to prevent men and women of character and discipline from contributing to the life of the nation. This is the basic distortion that is present in societies around the world.

Humanity today enjoys unmatched prosperity. However, we have also become captivated by our own ambitions, fantasies, and addictions, to an unprecedented degree. As we gratify our corporeal appetites, we succumb to the frenzy of life. We drink only to become thirstier; we eat only to become more gluttonous. We resort to financial manipulation to acquire more, selling our soul to the devil for pittance. Thus we drift away from the truth of human virtue.

As life is consumed in the pursuit of some transient material value, humanity ends up consuming itself and abandoning its dignity. In this state, there can be no immensity of faith, abundance of wisdom, or displays of love and spiritual delight. How could there be? Modern humanity evaluates life in only terms of comfort and enjoyment, completely neglecting the heavenly realities. We think only of how to accumulate more, what to buy or sell, and where to find pleasure. And when such ends cannot be lawfully achieved, we appeal to unlawful ones. When the visible ground of society ceases to serve our purposes, we move into the underground.

Today, humanity continues this dark, underground journey. But it is a dead-end we must abandon if we are to find our true path. Otherwise, an individual will drift from one distraction to another, never becoming himself. If rescued from communism, he will stumble into anarchism; if saved from atheism, he will adhere to monism; if freed from Darwinism, he will cling to Neo-Darwinism. He will suffer alienation, lose his identity, and be left to imitate others. In this way, humanity has wasted itself for centuries. We escaped from a political crisis only to fall into a moral one. We surmounted an economic crisis only to find ourselves in the midst of a military one. Moreover, our energies are depleted by our own negative attitudes. Deliverance from these misadventures will require a return to the traditional religious principles of belief, love, morality, metaphysical thinking, and spiritual training.

To believe is to know the truth as it is, and to love is to apply this knowledge to life. Those who do not believe can by no means understand the absolute truth, and those who do not love are like lifeless corpses. Belief is the most important source of action; it leads the spirit to engage with the whole of existence. Likewise, love is the most essential aspect of human thought. For this reason, those who would nurture our religious traditions should first turn to the altar of belief and ascend the pulpit of love. Their impact originates in their deep understanding of morality and virtue.

Morality is the essence of religion and a significant tenet of the divine message. If it is heroic to be moral and virtuous, then the Prophets and their sincere followers are the true heroes. The most apparent characteristic of Islam is morality. Anyone of discernment and wisdom can see that, verse by verse, chapter by chapter, the Qur'an and the Prophetic tradition are suffused with moral teaching. The Prophet, who embodied perfect morality, put this truth plainly when he said: "Islam is the beauty of character." As the Muslim community, we are the members of a moral system and the moral children of an epic story. No thought or fantasy could shake our morals, for we dream of attaining eternity through them. And we believe that our spiritual strength, which originates in metaphysical thought, will allow us to realize this dream.

Metaphysical thought denotes our effort to comprehend existence as the unity of its observable and unobservable aspects. Without this holistic embrace of both the intellect and the soul, everything crumbles into lifeless fragments. When we neglect metaphysical thought, we lose access to reason. All of history's great civilizations have been rooted in a tradition of metaphysical thought. This is especially true in the Islamic world, where successive civilizations have been established on the metaphysical foundation of the Qur'an. Metaphysical thought is the soul's penetration into nature, and those who attempt to oppose metaphysics with natural science foolishly attempt to turn a cascading river against the spring of its origin.

We can also define metaphysics as ability of love to perceive reality as a whole. In this respect, love finds all existence to be worthy of affection. The true lover pursues neither wealth nor fame. He breathes peacefully in the midst of the storms of love that burn in him. They hope to discern the visage of their Beloved in the face of annihilation, to perceive their Beloved among the scattered ashes of the existence, and to attain the unity of the lover and the Beloved, the seeker and the Sought One. They are always journeying from the valleys of "self-annihilation in God" (*fana fillah*) toward the heights of "self-permanence with God" (*baqa billah*), to use the Sufi terms. Surely, such a goal requires earnest spiritual training.

Spiritual training orients us to the purpose of our creation. It can also be defined as the way by which the spirit escapes the limits of corporeality, turns toward its origin, and fulfills the purpose of its creation.

The generations of our time have lost their spiritual dynamic and have become alienated to their essence. Poor, slovenly, and vagrant, they seem to be the victims of their own reasoning. We must help these generations to give their contemplation its proper object. And as their devoted servants, we believe that we can. Although our endeavors might be undervalued, we will not give up hope. We need only to nurture our will through worship and discipline it through self-criticism. If we fulfill our duty and walk on this way, then God will be there, wherever we turn. Our task is to spread these seeds across the golden hills of the future; it will be God who brings them to life.

We believe absolutely that, through the comprehensive effort of service, a new ethos of peace, security, and love can emerge out of the current world. We believe that humanity will find its true happiness, and that the future generations will place their trust in love rather than money, affluence, fame, position, and all kinds of greed. Then all will live according to the sovereignty of their hearts.

August 1995

Humanity Longing for Love

As humans, we have forgotten how to behave humanely. Our actions today hardly express the unique privilege of our position in existence. Despite possessing magnificent qualities, which even the angels envy, we engage in acts that would embarrass evil spirits. We are too often preoccupied with hatred, flushed with fury, and overcome with feelings of vengeance. Our hearts are without love, and the smog of enmity blankets our feelings. For too many years, we have lived unaware of the transforming influence of love.

Our thoughts constantly give rise to evil deeds. It has become second nature for us to destroy our environment, assimilating and suppressing everything "other." So many of us are controlled by our emotions at the expense of reason. We instinctively trample and silence those who do not think like us. Without considering alternate solutions to the problems we face, we plunge forward, enjoying only our own opinion. In this way, even our attempts at encouragement can become destructive. We do not win hearts or express ourselves in the tender language of the soul; these have become like outdated manners peculiar to the past. We work ourselves into a frenzy, facing the opposition that our own selfishness has engendered. If our rage is powerful enough, we crush our competitors. If it is not, then we do not hesitate to defame them, using any methods at our disposal.

In the world today, we can hear only the noise of oppressors and the cries of the oppressed. Countries have been suppressed, and victimized peoples have been groaning for many years. In many societies, all enthusiasm has been extinguished. Alienated from their own values, people have become like wolves to each other. Any difference in thought or understanding is considered cause for contention and conflict. People are set firmly against one another, and thus minor disagreements trigger irrepressibly violent fights. One man carves out another's eye, and so he responds with suicide bombers or vehicles loaded with explosives. There is savagery on every corner; we act like wild animals without a trace of humanity. Conscience, a mechanism that includes the will, mind, emotion, and heart, is paralyzed. The will pursues atrocious plots. The mind, once an observatory of the knowledge of God, has surrendered to our contaminated desires. Emotion, that pure spring of love, is made into a pit of snakes and scorpions. The heart, the window through which we contemplate the Truth, becomes like a tunnel with no light. It seems as if all of our uniquely human attributes have been alienated from their true purposes.

Although similar destruction and mischief has plagued humanity at each stage of history, our situation has been aggravated by the impact of globalization and technological advancement. On television, in magazines, and in newspapers, we see new horrors proclaimed every day. Even if we close our eyes and ears, the harrowing news unavoidably pierces us like a spear, causing incurable wounds in our hearts and souls. Sometimes we perceive a host of evils at once. We agonize with the victims of war in blood and tears and collapse with exhaustion as civilization collapses around us.

The wind of autumn seems to be blowing all around us, and people are like dry leaves. Everywhere we see:

> *Cities in ruin, homes devastated, communities with no leader,*
> *Bridges destroyed, canals demolished, roads with no traveler,*
> *Pitiful believers killing believers in the name of a "holy war,"*
> *Desolate dwellings, deserted villages, roofs collapsed,*
> *Days deprived of labor, evenings with no idea of tomorrow.*[22]

The tragedies that roil in us become screams, and we moan in the anguish of our helplessness. But the world waits for our help. It buckles in the face of humanity's indifference and unravels in the presence of our apathy. There are a few who hear and feel these cries, yet they themselves are too weak and powerless. And so in our day, humanity dies countless deaths, crying:

---

[22] Mehmed Akif (d. 1936).

Rains do not fall, nor do the tulips grow;
Will our fate always be the same?
Over this land of the divine mercy,
Even the winds of morning blow misery.[23]

In despair, one is tempted to say: "The crowds will always eat one another, and the masses will clash forever. People no longer love, nor extend a hand to the aggrieved, nor show compassion to the wronged. We are not safe anymore; the fate of the world will be determined by those madmen who think and speak of blood, and it will be an age of tyrants once again...."

However, this situation cannot continue, for this would mean the demise of humanity and its values. We have arrived at a historic intersection today. Let us lend an ear once again to the divine calls of the heroes of love and friendship, like Rumi and Yunus.[24] Come let us show the entire world what a privilege it is to be human. Let us proclaim "love" and "dialogue" in the days when hatred and animosity have darkened the face of the earth. Come, let us enlarge our conscience according to the divine mercy that encompasses all; let us open the gates of our hearts to all.

Let us no longer consider ourselves to be a drop destined to dry out and vanish. Instead, let us unite as one cascading river, flowing toward the ocean of eternity. We all are human: Our genes contain the trace of Adam, and our essence shares the truth of Ahmad.[25] Then let us stand against all evil and cry out to the universe that we are God's vicegerents on earth, and we are the candidates of eternity. Come let us make the angels once again envy our privilege. Let us walk together in our way toward God, hand in hand, heart to heart.

March 2008

---

[23] Suzi (d. 1830), Turkish-Ottoman Sufi poet.

[24] Yunus Emre (d. 1321), Turkish Sufi poet.

[25] As a Sufi concept, *al-haqiqa al-Ahmadiyya* or the truth of Ahmad denotes the primordial reality of Prophet Muhammad, peace and blessings be upon him, in the divine destiny. In Sufi understanding, this truth or reality is the ideal form of the human being and hence the essential norm of the divine creation.

Chapter Two

FAITH & WISDOM

The Love of God

In this dark time, the hearts of our people have succumbed to enmity. Our souls are sick, hatred is rampant, and people fight each other like wolves. In these inauspicious days, we need love and mercy even more than we need water and air; for we seem to have forgotten love, and compassion is like a word foreign to our tongues. We do not show mercy to our neighbors: Empathy has left us; our hearts are stubborn; hostility clouds our horizon; and everything appears to be black as coal. Quasi-tyrants stand on every corner, detesting tolerance, while many more curse dialogue. We invent new ways to denigrate each other with lies and slander; we express ourselves with teeth and claws, or with words that stink of blood.

There is a terrible disunity among individuals and among communities. When we speak, we place new emphasis on divisive words such as "we," "you," and "others." Our thirst for disintegration is never quenched. Continuous screaming matches play out on television like soap operas. We are disconnected from one another, and this separation is reflected in our all actions. Like the beads of a broken necklace, we are scattered here and there. We suffer from this disunity even more than we suffer from the work of tyrants.

In truth, these divisions among us are the result of our disconnection from God. We did not love Him with the devotion that His beauty and glory require, and thus He has let love die away in our souls. Now deprived of Him, our empty hearts snarl at each other with egotism. We label each other "reactionary," "bigoted," or "infidel" in our unceasing war. It is as if we have been cursed: Love has left us destitute, and we hunger for mercy and kindness. However, since we did not love God, He has allowed love and respect to leave our hearts. If we turn to Him even now, He will give us love again. But we are far from the true source of love, and the paths we are on do not lead to Him.

The rain of love does not fall on our souls, although it once came in downpours, and our hearts have become deserts. Only our love for God can remedy these ailments.

The love of God is the beginning of every good thing and the pure source of all other love. Love and compassion enter our hearts only by His will. And when we are secure in our relationship with Him, all our other bonds will be made stronger. The love of God is our faith and religion; we cannot live without it. God's love is the essence of existence, and through it existence will be nurtured into a form of Paradise. God created everything in accordance with love, and because of His love, He has established a relationship with humanity.

Love is manifest in the spirit, not in corporeal things. Wherever we might direct our love, it always turns to face God, even if we have confused our Beloved with some fleeting thing. But when our love finds its proper object, then it is raised to its true value. Then we escape the dissipation that accompanies our desire and worship nothing other than God. And only then will we remain with those who walk on the right path, in a right relationship with all existence.

Idolaters think that what they worship is a deity simply because they worship it. But God is worshipped and loved according to His unique and eternal divinity. His lordship requires our service, so we serve Him at all times. We are always expressing our love for Him, giving Him thanks for our attainments, and seeking to manifest our loyalty in every action. Many things inspire "figurative" love: beauty, perfection, majesty, wealth, power, status, prosperity, and family.[26] But excessive love for such things can cause us to associate partners with God, a deviation that leads to idolatry. Then we become captivated by beauty and stature. We applaud perfection and bow down before majesty. We sacrifice our humanity and freedom for the sake of wealth and power, or we debase ourselves in the flattery of prosperity and status. In this way, we distribute among many helpless creatures the love that should be given to the One who provides us with such bounties and gifts. Only He is the rightful owner of beauty and perfection, the

---

[26] In Sufism, only the love of God is real; all other kinds are figurative.

majestic king, and the absolutely rich and powerful. When we love created things more than the Creator himself, we spend the precious jewel of our love in vain, and suffer from the indifference and unfaithfulness of our false beloveds.

The believer loves God first, and loves all others for His sake. He values the things of this world for the divine manifestations revealed in them. The believer admires them and proclaims his love for them in God's name. A love that does not take God into consideration is dispersed, unpromising, unstable, and fruitless. Therefore, we should love God before all else, and should love all other things because they manifest His names and attributes. We should embrace all creation with respect, and in the face of every blessing say: "This too is from You." Then every blessing will be a moment of union with the Beloved. But for this, we will need hearts that are pure as a house of God and tongues that are trained to recite the divine manifestations that shine in the faces of all created things.

> *Wishing to see her beauty in many faces,*
> *The lover should be in pieces, like a broken mirror.*[27]

For those who can see, every creature is a shining mirror, or a eulogy in verse, that reflects the glory of the Creator. The human face expresses the mysterious truth of divine mercy:

> *God made you a mirror for Himself,*
> *A looking glass for His unique self.*[28]

These words are an important reminder of our position in the universe. Since humanity is the mysterious mirror of the hidden beauty of the Divine, our gaze should be fixed on Him. And as we observe His manifestations, we anticipate His benevolence that will lead us further into the country of love. In order to attain His love and pleasure, we should continue in closeness to Him, our hearts turning like the keys that will unlock His "hidden treasure."[29]

---

[27] Anonymous couplet from classical Turkish poetry.
[28] Hakani Mehmed Bey (d. 1606), Turkish-Ottoman poet.
[29] In Sufism, God's eternal beauty, which was unknown before creation, is referred to as the "hidden treasure."

If love is like Solomon, and the heart its miraculous throne, then whenever love is seated in the heart, it will be raised up.[30] And it is certain that the king will ascend his throne, sooner or later. Once the throne of our heart has found its Solomon, then it will always be devoted to God. We will converse with Him in contemplation and perceive our every action, our very drinking and breathing, as a dispensation of His blessings. Our time will be spent in the warmth of His closeness, and then our hearts will begin to burn like furnaces with the flames of love and longing. We recognize that our love is a gift from God, so we never reveal the agony of our longing to the ignorant who do not understand.

This road is open to all; the only condition is that the traveler be sincere and determined. If we see and understand that all beauty, perfection, greatness and magnificence belong to God, then we should passionately turn to Him with a love that befits His glory. As long as this ardent love is directed solely to God, it will unify our feelings. In fact, love causes no deviation in a heart dedicated to the divine unity and devoted to the precepts of Islam. The person who believes in divine unity loves God for His own sake, and this love does not expect anything in return, neither from this world nor the next. As feelings pour from the springs of his heart, the believer filters and tests them according to the principles of the Qur'an and the teachings of the Prophet, peace and blessings be upon him. Thus, he is kept on the proper path, even when human excitements overwhelm him; his path is straight, even when he is consumed with the fire of love.[31] Such a believer loves God deeply, and respects His absolute sublimity and transcendence by acknowledging Him as the true Owner and Master of everything. He acknowledges that God is to be known by His names and defined by His attributes. So his love never misleads him into erratic sentiment.

---

[30] The author refers to an image found in a couplet of Muhammed Lütfi, which compares love to Solomon, and the heart to his throne. In Islamic narrative, Solomon had his throne fly miraculously.

[31] The author implicitly refers to the particular tradition of the so-called "intoxicated" Sufis, who claim divinity out of the joy and excitement of being "united" with God.

The one who believes in divine unity sets his heart on God. He loves, seeks, and worships God before everything. Every action expresses his desire and his service. Consequently, he loves the Prophets and eminent friends of God, who are the purest mirrors of His manifestations, as well as the special servants of God, who represent His will as exceptional "vicegerents" on earth. Among them, Prophet Muhammad, the Pride of Humanity, peace and blessings be upon him, is most deserving of love, for he is the focus of God's favors, His devout apostle, the true interpreter of His Names and Attributes, and the last and most noble of the Prophets. It is for God's sake that the believer loves youth, which He bestows in order that we fully experience our temporality. It is for God's sake that the believer loves this world, where God manifests His beautiful names and attributes and where we cultivate the good things that will be harvested in the other world. The believer loves parents, who are heroes of compassion when they care for their children, and all family members who share with him the same divine blessings. These loves are also the expressions of a sincere love of God; the believer loves all things for His sake.

As believers, we open our hearts to our beloved ones for God's sake, but unbelievers love them as if they were loving God himself. These two loves are completely different. To love something for the sake of God is a sacred act that originates in faith, relates to worship, and manifests itself as moral conduct. It is the mark of the perfect believer. In contrast to the sensual love—if it can be called "love" at all—which expresses the animal inclinations of our nature, love that begins in God is like a sacred drink that the angels rush to taste. If we give all our existence to the Beloved in such love, leaving nothing for ourselves, then only concern with the Beloved remains in our heart. The heart then adjusts its rhythm and burns with a new longing, while our eyes attempt to cool these flames with tears. The heart reproaches the eyes for revealing its secret, as it strives to hide its suffering from outsiders even as it burns within. It murmurs:

If you are in love, grieve not over its sting;
Do not let others know of your agony.[32]

Love is a sovereign that has made its throne in our hearts. It speaks in the groans of hope and longing that we pour out to God on the prayer-rug in solitude. The expressions of the suffering of love should be kept hidden from others, especially from those ignorant of it. If love is for the Beloved who is All-Knowing, then it should remain in the most private sphere, away from the eyes of strangers.

Childish people will advertise their little loves everywhere they go, complaining loudly of their sufferings and making sure that their beloved is the talk of the town. But the lovers of God are quiet and sincere. They put their head on the threshold of His presence, pour out their heart to Him, and may even faint from passion; but they never reveal the secret agony of their love. They put their hands and feet at His service, and their ears and tongue at His command. Their heart waits at the horizon for the divine manifestations to rise like the sun. They melt in the light of His existence, annihilated in their love. As they feel Him more deeply, they burn with love and say, "More!" They drink the wine of love cup after cup and say, "More!" They are never satisfied with loving and being loved, so they repeat, "More!"

As they continue asking for more, the Beloved unveils to them unprecedented beauties and removes the curtains from many mysteries. Then they feel and think only of Him, and they see the manifestations of His unimaginable beauty in everything. They dissolve their own will and power into His, expressing their love in obedience and fidelity. The doors of their heart are bolted against distractions so securely that no other beloved can enter their "prosperous home."[33] They turn to God with all of their existence, and their praises to Him come from far beyond the horizon of even their own comprehension. They fully hope that God will honor their faithfulness. They understand that their position in God's sight is related to the position they

---

[32] Anonymous couplet from classical Turkish Sufi poetry.

[33] Here the author compares the heart to *al-bayt al-maʿmur*, the angels' house of worship in heaven, which is traditionally considered the heavenly counterpart of Kaʿba. (*See* Qur'an, 52:4)

dedicate to Him in their own, so they strive to stand upright in His presence.

Although they love Him madly, they do not lay claim to anything. Instead, they are as embarrassed and loyal as a debtor, echoing the words of Rabi'a al-Adawiyya: "I swear that I have not worshipped You in order to demand Paradise; the only reason for my service is that I love You." They travel toward His sublime presence with nothing but an upwelling love, and they constantly thank Him for His bounties to them along the way. Their hearts are close to Him, while their minds reflect upon all creation. They hear the sounds of love in everything; they are enraptured with the scent of love that arises from every flower; and every scene reflects to them His beauty. In his presence, they always talk and think of love. All creation is displayed before them as a festival of God's love, and they hear in it the divine harmony.

Once love has established its authority in the heart, opposites begin to resemble each other. Presence and absence, blessing and adversity, ease and hardship, pleasure and pain: all give the same sound and look the same way. For the lover sees suffering no different from enjoyment, and disease no different from remedy. He tastes anguish like it is spring water. No matter how ruthless existence might be, he holds his position with profound fidelity. His gaze is fixed on the door that will be opened to him. He keeps watch for divine favors and manifestations, ready to welcome them. His obedience is the utmost expression of his love, and his heart beats with the joy of submission. He trembles like a leaf for the fear of disobeying his Beloved and begs Him for help in order not to fall. In time, this quest for the utmost unity with his Beloved makes him loved both in the heavens and on the earth. He only considers God and expects nothing in return for his love; for this would be a betrayal of his love, even if his expectations were for the other world. Yet he considers it disrespectful to reject the favors of the Beloved when they come without his asking. He accepts them in total humility, and takes refuge from their temptations in Him.

For the lover, longing itself is the highest honor, and self-annihilation in the will of the Beloved is the highest attainment. Love initially requires repentance, attention, and patience, and it grows with passion, yearning, familiarity, satisfaction, and prudence. The path of love requires that we be purified from personal desires. It demands that we relate all our thoughts to the Beloved, remain steadfast in our memory of Him, and hope always in the expressions of His love. On this path, to love to an utmost degree is *ishq*, to gush with passion and joy is *shawq*, to welcome gladly every treatment of the Beloved is *rida*, and to practice constant prudence and sobriety against the ecstatic feelings of being in His presence is *tamkin*.[34]

As these qualities dominate his heart, the lover displays peculiar attitudes. At times, he seeks solitude in which to cry and unburden his heart to God. At times, he delves deep into various considerations and has conversations with Him. Sometimes he mourns over his separation from God; sometimes he is relieved by the hope of reunion and calmed by tears of joy. He often tastes the unique presence of God in the midst of creation's multiplicity and forgets what is happening around him. Sometimes, he disappears so completely into the awe of the divine presence that he no longer hears his own voice and breath.

Our spiritual knowledge of God is the ground in which love grows and is nourished. One who is deprived of wisdom cannot truly love, just as one whose senses are deadened cannot attain wisdom. Sometimes God stimulates our hearts to revive love in us; this is a special bestowal that we can only anticipate. However, such a passive waiting for extraordinary favor is less meaningful than the active anticipation that strives for wisdom and knowledge of God. Faithful servants base their expectations on their actions. Theirs is a dynamic stance, which impels them toward marvelous activity. These are the loyal lovers. No matter how their Beloved treats them, they are glad. With fidelity they can say:

> *I am a helpless lover, my dear; I will never abandon you.*
> *Rend my heart with a dagger if you will, but I will never leave you.*[35]

They suffer, longing for reunion with the Beloved, but they never complain. They always dream of reuniting with the Beloved. Every

---

[34] These are essential Sufi concepts regarding one's relationship with God.

[35] Nesimi (d. 1417), Turkmen Sufi poet.

conversation they have is about Him. With His name always on their lips, they reach angelic heights.

Love is their soul, and for them, the soul governs the body. They can survive without their body, but not without this soul. There is no room in their existence for anything except this love. Even if they appear in this world as the poorest and weakest, they stand high enough in the spiritual realm to crown the kings. They are great in their weakness, powerful in their frailty, and boundlessly wealthy despite their poverty. They may look like dim candles, but they are a source of energy rich enough to fuel the sun. And although all people appeal to them in respect and admiration, they appeal to no one but God. Their richness of soul exceeds the universe, yet when they turn toward God, they become like a tiny spark, a nothing:

> *The candle of the soul has such a flame*
> *That cannot fit in the lantern of the firmament.*[36]

They cannot imagine life without the Beloved; it is not a life at all. For them, to live without this love is to waste their life. Any pleasure or joy that does not relate to Him is a distraction. They consider those who are without love to be strangers to the true life of humanity.

June and July 2003

---

[36] Sheikh Galib (d. 1798), Turkish-Ottoman Sufi poet.

The Believer Standing before God

The believer, with his rich spiritual life, is confident in his future, and his faith inspires trust in all who encounter him. He stands as steadfast as a monument. Aware that all of his works are seen by God, he always acts with enviable refinement and courtesy. The believer is kind, decent, gentle and polite before God and before others. Even if his life is threatened or he faces fierce oppression, he never resorts to any rudeness.

The exceptional eloquence and profundity in the soul of the believer are the result of service to God. He is remarkably kind and attentive, fully mindful of his speech and action, and serious in all matters. But at the same time, he is very mild and generous, with a heart that is open to all. His inner world has been enriched and enlarged by faith, so he embraces everyone, offering them bowls of love and compassion and revealing to them the beauties of closeness with God. At times, he dreams of the day he will encounter God with joy. And at other times, he worries over the Day of Judgment with deep awe and fear.

Great-hearted, the believer sees through the smog of hatred around him and ignores the storms aroused by jealousy and slander. He disregards the distress and annoyance that such things cause in his soul. For he stands in the presence of God, and this reality clears all improprieties from his mind and purifies his inner world. There can be no defect in his soul, for in inwardness, he enjoys the spiritual gifts of the realms beyond. He behaves according to this spiritual depth, and his goal is too lofty for him to be distracted by anything. His faith is complete, he respects his elders and cherishes the young with compassion, and he orders his life according to the virtues that have been bestowed to him.

He rejects anything that does not express his ideal of service to humanity: confused thoughts, futile actions, and vain words that do not ultimately lead to God. His silence is contemplative, and his speech always proclaims the lofty concepts of God. His external and internal senses are fixed upon God; he is as pure in his devotion as the angels. He is always ready to soar, glowing with spiritual enthusiasm. Because of his respect for God, his ultimate purpose, he does not insist on his own way as if it were his goal. He always sets his eyes upon what is beyond the horizon. His effort, passion, and diligence resound throughout the world, and these values are the true motifs of his life.

In his fleeting days, the believer manages to both develop this world and attain the next. He does not waste his natural and spiritual capacities, the divine gifts granted to him at birth, and he does not waste time with trivialities that have no consequence for this world or the next. In service, he easily gives away all that God has entrusted to him and does not let a single penny of God's blessing go to waste. He works and earns in the way that is right and lawful, so that his efforts may join the cascading rivers of Paradise. To this end, the believer always acts in the name of God and for His pleasure, giving careful thought to all that he does. He seeks the abundance of the ocean in the smallest drop and searches for the blessings of the sun in the atom, perpetually striving to see the eternal in transient things.

He loves everyone and everything for God's sake. He breathes with love at all times, forming an atmosphere of love around himself. He rushes to stop the cries of mourning wherever he hears them, and he applies balm to the afflictions of others. He turns tears into laughter, helpless moans into praises to God, and storms of fire into the breezes of divine grace. He suffers so that others may not suffer. His tears flow so that others may not weep. If he does not serve others, he considers himself worthless. Selfless and altruistic, he always prefers "us" to "me." A man of spirit and meaning, he does not allow his heart to be choked out by corporeal demands, or his soul to be overwhelmed by the desires of his body. The believer pursues the kind of integrity and innocence exemplified by the Prophets. He is a champion of self-discipline, contenting himself with lawful pleasures. He gives his willpower its due as he struggles against corporeal desires.

He overcomes all obstacles by God's help, and reaches the horizon of his soul without difficulty.

He is serious, diligent, and determined to represent goodness and overcome evil. At times, he is so diligent that he is in competition with the angels, who once again praise God for creating humankind.[37] He wins angelic admiration by applying the divine gifts granted to him at birth only toward their created purpose. In doing so, he acts as a reliable steward of all that has been entrusted to him, and God honors him with His presence.

Every individual is entrusted with existence and bestowed with universal human virtues. The aspiration for Paradise, the capacity for attaining it, and the ability to contemplate God's beauty are other special endowments. All these have been granted to humanity to be used in conformity with their purposes, which the Creator has determined. From this perspective, to misuse human potential and live under the rule of corporeality is to disrespect and betray the divine gifts, which can only delight the evil spirits and embarrass the angels. Therefore, the believer recognizes that God's initial gifts are the means by which we attain His subsequent blessings. In utilizing them, he realizes his true identity as a servant.

On the contrary, those who do not believe—who do not recognize their divine gifts or enlist them in the cause of faith, wisdom, and love—will be deprived of the subsequent and everlasting blessings. And, since they neglect their life to come, they can never be fully happy in this life. They suffer from worry and distress, depression and paranoia, as a result of their disbelief. In this way, they turn this beautiful world, this luminous passageway to the realms beyond, into a hell for themselves. Those who do not believe cannot truly love other people. They find themselves hating others for insignificant reasons, and they receive hatred in return. Most of the time, they suffer from greed and avarice, are frustrated by disappointment, and tremble with

---

[37] The author refers to the Qur'anic narrative that the angels, having understood the superior character of Adam, started to praise God, saying: *"May You be glorified! We have knowledge only of what You have taught us. You are the All-Knowing and All-Wise."* (Qur'an, 2:32)

fear of death. In a frantic state, they begin to confuse white with black, good with bad. They consider those who do not think like them to be enemies and traitors, and thus they become obsessed with nightmares of distrust. In short, the hellish afflictions they suffer are the poisonous effects of their disbelief.

As for the true believer, he receives the gifts of God so abundantly it is as if he receives the harvest of countless grains.[38] He utilizes the divine gifts as stairs with which to ascend toward God, or as a ramp that leads to the horizon of His good pleasure. And he proceeds together with the people of Paradise, comforted by the signs of his coming attainment of God's pleasure in Paradise.

May 2006

---

[38] A reference to the Qur'anic verse: *"Those who spend their wealth in God's cause are like grains of corn that produce seven ears, each bearing a hundred grains. God multiplies for whom He wills. God is All-Embracing (with His mercy), All-Knowing."* (2:261)

The Characteristics of a Believer

Today, we need responsible generations who are vigorous in the awareness of their duty toward God more than ever. We need ideal people who will guide our society: the guides who will help us escape from the abyss of ignorance and anarchy and lead us to faith, wisdom, integrity, and peace. Humanity has managed to stitch new garments out of its own death shroud before, and we can thank these exceptional minds and souls for our past rejuvenation. In every time of crisis, they are the ones who illuminate the way and attend to the crowds who suffer from economic, intellectual, religious, and moral depression. Thanks to them, we can continually reinterpret our existence, thus dissolving obstacles in our thoughts and feelings. Thanks to them, we have re-construed the world of phenomena around us all over again. They recite the book of existence to us melodiously after it has lost its meaning. Thus we are able to analyze it again, chapter by chapter and line by line. Thanks to them, the universe becomes an exhibition of wonder to us again, and we rediscover the hidden truths.

These auspicious people are characterized by their faith and by their effort to represent this faith everywhere. They believe that, with this faith and effort, they can surmount everything and attain God's good pleasure, the truest peace. Then after turning this world into a paradise, they will settle into the Paradise beyond this life. In the assurance of their joyful end, they travel through life as if they were traveling through the slopes of Paradise.

Although the degree of faith may differ from person to person, faith has always been the most influential dimension of humanity's life. No system of thought, doctrine, or philosophy can match its positive impact. When faith enters a person's heart, it transforms the way he thinks about God, the universe, and his own life. His gaze becomes so encompassing that he can survey the whole of existence as if he

were perusing a book, page by page. The creation that he had once
taken for granted, all those phenomena that had been dead and meaningless in his mind, are suddenly vitalized. They become his friends
and companions, welcoming him in compassion. In this warm atmosphere, he senses the true value of his life. The believer comprehends
that humanity is the only form of consciousness present among creation.
He walks the secret paths that meander throughout the universe and
perceives the mysteries behind the veil of all phenomena. Then he is set
free from the narrow confines of three-dimensional space and finds himself in the immensities of the infinite.

Every believer, thanks to the flux of thoughts in the depths of his
soul, enjoys the infinite in the midst of the temporal world according
to the degree of his faith. Although the believer lives within the limits
of space and time, he becomes as free and pure as the absolute, reaching the status of the lofty beings and listening to the melodies of angels.
Created from a drop of fluid, he flourishes when he nurtures the "divine
breath" contained in his soul.[39] And no matter how small he may appear
to be, the believer is a transcendent being that neither the earth nor
the sky can contain. He attains spiritual qualities as immense and endless as the heavens. The believer may walk among us, sit with us, and
worship as we do, but he is vaulted to divine heights by the humble
position of his prostration. He beats his wings in the same sky as the
lofty spirits, experiencing the other world in this one.

Such a believer transcends his individuality as he dedicates himself to human virtue, and thus attains universality. He embraces all
believers, lends a hand to everyone, and greets the whole of existence
with sincerity. In everything and everyone, he recognizes the traces of
the divine manifestations. He delves so deep into meditation that he
can almost hear the beating wings of the angels. From the fearsome
thunder of the lightning to the soothing melodies of the birds, from
the gorgeous waves of the oceans to the eternal murmurs of the rivers, from the eerie roar of the forests to the awe-inspiring song of the

---

[39] The Qur'an teaches that when God creates the human individual in the womb, He
breathes from His own "spirit" into the created body. This divine spirit constitutes
our soul, the essence of human identity. (*See* Qur'an 32:9)

summits, he is surrounded by this panoply of beauties and says, "This is truly life!" He joins with all creation to voice the truth. Through prayers and praises, he raises his breaths to the dignity of their true value.

In constant humility, he waits like a servant at the door of the Divine, hoping that it will open onto God's familiar gaze. He waits for the fortunate hour when absence and separation will disappear and peace and nearness will envelop his soul. He yearns to satisfy his desire for reunion. But even as he travels toward God, sometimes flying through the sky, sometimes running on the ground, he does not neglect creation, his companion. He experiences a new reunion with God at every turn and extinguishes the fire of longing, but it is quickly rekindled with a new spark. Who knows how many times a day he feels the breezes of divine friendship? Or how often he feels a deep sadness over the loneliness and affliction of those deprived of such blessings?

Indeed, the believer with such a broad horizon feels exceptionally ardent and resolute as he sets out to explore new realms. He thinks of the future honors and achievements on which he will be able to put his signature, thanks to God's providence. And so he never tires, but keeps running with his path open before him, his will free, and his heart at peace. At every moment, his existential curiosity grows. His soul is at rest in a never-ending field of peace. Unlike many others, he never faces loneliness or alienation; for he knows where he comes from and is confident in his purpose. He knows where he is going and is aware of the wisdom that governs all of the gatherings and dispersions of the world. He feels neither the weariness of the road nor the fears, worries, and afflictions of others. He trusts in God, leaps with hope, and tastes the joy of the summit in his dreams of Paradise.

According to the degree of their faith, such heroic believers can travel even the most difficult roads as if they were promenading through the slopes of Paradise. Because of their relationship with God, they challenge the whole universe and surmount every difficulty. They are not terrified of calamities or destruction, and they do not flee from even the most terrifying situations. They hold their head high, bowing to no one except God. Such believers do not fear anybody, do not expect to be rewarded by anybody, and are not indebted to anybody. When they achieve victory, they guard themselves against temptation and at the same time are humbled with gratitude and relieved with the tears of joy. When they lose, they are patient and determined, and they launch out again with a sharpened will. They do not become arrogant and ungrateful in the face of blessing or fall into despair when suffering deprivation.

In their relationships with others, believers have hearts like those of the Prophets. They love everything and embrace everyone. They turn a blind eye to the faults of others but question themselves for their smallest mistakes. They forgive the wrongs of those around them, even when they feel angered, and know how to get along with even the most acrimonious people. Islam advises its adherents to forgive as often as possible and to avoid the traps of hatred and revenge. Those who are conscious of their constant progress toward God could behave in no other way. They always have good wishes for others and seek the goodness of others. They keep love alive in their soul, and maintain an endless war against hatred and animosity. The fire of their penitence purifies them of all faults and wrongs. They constantly wrestle with the evil feelings of their nature and prepare the ground for goodness and beauty by first making their own hearts good and beautiful. Like Rabi'a al-Adawiyya, they receive everything, even poison, as if it were a sweet drink. They welcome everyone with smiles, even those who approach them with hatred. They repel the most aggressive armies with the invincible armor of love.

God loves them, and they love God. They are always filled with the excitement of loving and are enraptured by the feeling of being loved. With humility and tenderness, they make themselves like the soil in which roses can grow. They are respectful to others, but also protect their honor, which is more valuable to them than this temporal life. They do not let their tolerance, compassion, and gentleness be interpreted as weakness; they live according to their beliefs and do not heed the censures or praises of people. Instead, they care only that the atlas of their thoughts not lose its color; for they have resolved to be true believers.

May 1999

The Purpose of Life

Whether we consider this life worth enduring in all its hardship depends to a large extent on whether we have confidence in its purpose. We are often reminded of the mystery of life, especially when we reflect upon our own humanity. And as we continue this contemplation throughout the years of our life, this enigma is slowly and gradually resolved.

But creation's primary purpose is obvious: Considering the ways in which humanity, the universe, and God are intertwined, we can say that our purpose is to embody the ideals of faith, wisdom, and spiritual delight, and thus demonstrate the privilege of being human. The realization of such a great project demands systematic thinking and disciplined action. To clarify, we take the first step toward realizing this purpose when we initiate the virtuous cycle of "thought and action." In this cycle, our thoughts generate further actions, which, in turn, generate more subtle and complex thoughts, according to the spiritual perception of our hearts and the reflection of our intellect.

Undoubtedly, this process requires strong belief, conscious behavior, and complete self-control in every action. Whoever has these characteristics will reflect upon the currents of life in order to understand their meaning, even though others submit to them heedlessly, even unconsciously. The former turn their thoughts into actions, which are enriched by their intellectual labor. They suffer the birth pangs of a new idea every day, for they believe that only the mind straining at its limits is productive. They are convinced that the greater the pains of thought and more restless the soul, the stronger, more consistent, and more brilliant will be the ideas born in the womb of that mind. Every day they scrutinize existence over again, embroidering it in the lacework of their thoughts. The wisdom embedded in the soul of the universe necessitates such a rigorous endeavor.

Most importantly, our existence must be appreciated as the threshold of the world of blessings. We exist within a world of bounties, and our duty is to utilize them, making them rungs upon the ladder that leads to higher blessings. We invite God's providence by first giving our willpower its due, thus proving ourselves to be unique among creation. Our duty is to contemplate our position within the flux of existence and reflect upon our relationships; our spiritual intellect will then become a source of wisdom for us. If we do this, we will see ourselves differently and perceive ourselves more deeply: We will learn that phenomena are articulate and have much to teach us.

Here is the horizon one must reach in order to attain true life. We are the most important among the living elements of the universe. We are the soul of the universe, its essence and extract, from which the whole of existence has expanded and flourished. Our essential responsibility is then to read and evaluate all the pages of the book of existence from this profound perspective, uncovering the wisdom at work in the depths of our souls. It is our responsibility to escape the turmoil of corporeal life, that period of suffering between birth and death, and to live in the depths of our heart, where we can search out the divine manifestations and spiritual delights.

In fact, what makes this often worrisome and painful life worth living are the divine gifts that we attain at every stage of our temporal journey. Those who are exhilarated by these gifts are enraptured without fail by the divine manifestations. As they savor such spiritual pleasures, they run toward God like a poem that flows excitedly toward its finale.

Our happiness does not depend on external gratification and is thus not subject to cessation. Ours is the everlasting happiness that emanates from our own souls, the happiness that is enriched by our connection to God and results in Paradise. Indeed this is the joy that wells up within us and spreads over our whole existence. Our inner world is a panorama of the manifestations of God's generosity; our conscience never tires in its pursuit of them; our life passes in lying in wait for them; our eyes look to the horizon of our fortune to welcome with celebration even the slightest signs of divine acceptance; and our soul expresses its delight with hymns:

> *You have ascended the throne of my heart.*
> *O my King, here you are welcome!* [40]

Today, we need guides who will raise new generations to such understanding. The younger generations, following these heroic guides, will live their youth fully in accordance with its purpose. Beyond the horizons where their souls will be unified with the infinite, they will perceive that mortality is identical to eternal life. They will wonder at the worlds of beauty contained in every fleeting moment of life and obtain a new understanding of infinity by discerning its color in the face of each thing. They will then understand that this life is really worth living. With this understanding, they will travel through the depths of their soul as if through galaxies and will experience the rich dimensions of this temporal life.

July 1997

---

[40] Muhammed Lütfi (d. 1956), Turkish Sufi master and poet. Also known as Alvarlı Efe, he was one of the teachers of Fethullah Gülen.

The Love of Truth

Truth simply means the essence and reality of things. To know the truth is to know clearly what a thing is, what it means, and what it signifies beyond its appearance. What is the essence and reality of the human being or the universe? What do they mean, both as individuals and when taken as a whole? What is there beyond existence and the beauty and harmony manifest in it: beyond the atoms and nebulas, beyond the material and spiritual depths of humanity? Creation cannot be the result of coincidence; there must be a truth upon which everything—from particles to planets—depends. There is certainly an ultimate basis for everything, and every human individual has a duty to know this truth. To pursue this obligation with zeal and concern is to know the love of truth.

Such a love searches all existence for the essence of reality; this is the surest way to reach the Truth of all truths. We first feel the stirrings of this love of truth in the excitement and passion of our spiritual life, in the curiosity with which we seek out the meaning beyond every appearance, and in the animation of our will. Then, we evaluate the outer and inner worlds in the joy and solemnity of worship, reviewing phenomena from the perspective of ever-changing scientific paradigms. We endure the difficulties of intellectual work, resist despair or panic when faced with seemingly inextricable problems, and make the attainment of truth our ultimate goal, no matter what the cost.

This journey can also be characterized as a pondering: a reflection and evaluation of phenomena according to their premises and consequences. It is a comprehensive contemplation and a diligent scrutiny that tests everything within the horizon of our understanding. And it endures against the maddening persistence of time, tirelessly waiting for the divine fulfillment.

If we face the universe in this way, in the love of truth, then everything begins to proclaim its meaning; objects unburden themselves of their secrets, giving light to our horizon and relief to our hearts. The amazing dynamism and fascinating harmony of electrons, the precise movements of molecules, the perfect structure of the cell: all provide inexhaustible insights to those who examine them. Our organs with their countless functions, the mind with its myriad activities, our conscience in all its profundity, the faith and love of humanity, our yearning for union with the Creator, the abundance of the creatures on land and sea: our souls are enlivened by the study of these as we progress toward the truth. The earth provides the conditions and resources necessary to life; the sun dazzles with its energy and presents itself to every creature on earth; the cosmos, macro and micro, pulse with their own majesty; and all of them send out messages in the name of truth.

The earth, which we see and observe every day, excites our hearts with the love of truth. For it is more beautiful than any spectacle, more magnificent than any palace, more informative than any teacher, more orderly than the most careful system, and more fascinating than the most brilliant promenades. The earth is always fresh and colorful: It is the picture of, and the enchanting doorway to, Paradise.

If we reflect on nature and existence without prejudice, we cannot help but admire every creature we encounter, and we will dream of the essence of existence like a lover dreams for the beloved. With each new scrutiny and analysis, we will become curious researchers and loving discoverers of the truth beyond all beings. Every curious and prudent mind that interprets the universe in this manner will view life differently, and the colors, patterns, and textures of creation will transform into praise before his eyes. In spiritual ecstasy, he will observe the heavens and the earth with enchantment. Every sound, from the roar of thunder to the melodies of birds, becomes for him a hymn that glorifies the Creative Almighty. He experiences spiritual delight in all phenomena, from the changes of weather to the murmuring of rivers. As he experiences God's infinite power and compassion in all phenomena, he becomes as joyful as a child. Like a curious student approaching the truth, or like a lover sensing the nearness of the beloved, he is always hopeful. He says "not yet" and continues on in his search, comprehending in all things the immense truths that books cannot express.

One day, he will come to know that the Supreme Being, who is beyond our comprehension and descriptions, is manifest in the sound, breath, color, pattern, form, and spirit of all that he sees. Then the eternal harmony will resonate in his intuition, and he will continue even further, reaching the horizon beyond which everything recites: "God is the Worshipped One. God is the Intended One. God is the Beloved One ...."

For such a vigilant spirit, all existence is a display of beauties, a gallery of marvels, and a promenade of pleasure and delight. Those who see with the eyes of their hearts, who view the world in the light of faith, are already walking on the paths of Paradise. They often swoon with the ecstasy of the eternal truth, and they let their insight direct their journey. These lovers of truth are welcomed by all creation to receive special lessons of wisdom. They travel from one valley to another, drinking up the knowledge and love offered by each creature. They salute everything and are saluted by everything. With every step, they come closer to the Truth of all truths. They receive messages from God with the help of their faith and wisdom, aware that they have been bestowed with special favors. When the time comes, the lovers of truth will reach the horizon of divine contemplation, where they will see the invisible things and hear the unheard things. And in their perfect pleasure, enthusiasm, and awe, they will never wish to leave the serenity of such contemplation.

This love of truth generates a zeal for scientific research, another important subject that requires separate treatment.

May 2004

CHAPTER THREE

MORALS & SPIRITUALITY

The Heart

Love is like Solomon,
Borne aloft on the heart, its throne.[41]

The heart is humanity's most essential feature and its greatest treasure. It is the expression of our spiritual existence, the source of our feelings and beliefs, and the pathway to our soul's ultimate depths. Those who walk on the path of the heart will not experience any darkness, and those who soar on the wings of their hearts will surmount any obstacle. Human virtues are cultivated on the hillsides of the heart; faith, love, and spiritual pleasures are the fruits of its garden.

If your heart is like a desert, your thoughts and feelings will inevitably wither and fade. In our history, human reason enjoyed its golden age when it submitted to the rule of the heart. Under the heart's guardianship, reason left behind countless immortal works. In those times, matter was melted and re-forged in the furnace of our spiritual essence. Then, our experience became a fairground of the Hereafter, this world intermingled with the next, and the treasures of the transcendent realms were offered here. It is according to the measures of the other world that the objects of this one become priceless. In those times, the sugar was separated from the cane, the bud was pregnant with a flower, and the soil was imbued with the lights of the other world. Things of this world found fulfillment and were perfected. The tulips and lilies of the earth began to dance in the presence of the heart, and the charms of the next world were felt in every corner.

But we gave our minds to idle gossip, and our reason gave way to deceit. As the tongue of conscience and the melodies of the heart fell

---

[41] Muhammed Lütfi (d. 1956).

silent, the earth became like a graveyard, and our homes like coffins. Life became a drudgery, and our spirits were stifled by the smog of our misplaced longing. In such malaise, carnal feelings and corporeal thoughts ambush our souls like bandits. They present us with various poisons, and we become a deluded crowd: a mob that cannot hear the voice of conscience and is closed to reason, that contemplates and understands nothing.

Today, we yearn for the stories of the heart, for in them we feel the reviving breaths of Jesus.[42] Since the beginning of the world, the people of the heart have always been the fortunate ones, traveling in the realms beyond the heavens with wings like angels. These heroes transcend the limits of their bodies to hold the reins of both worlds. While others beg from door to door, they live among the blessings of Paradise with contentment. The dust and the grime of this world do not blacken their horizon, nor does the colorful attraction of the Hereafter distract them from their purpose. In every deed, they enjoy the friendship of God, thus their devotion is the most profitable trade.[43] They faithfully realize their heart's purpose in a way that befits humanity. These fortunate ones sing of their love in the eternal melodies, raising their voices to the furthest galaxies.

The heart is the intersection of God's grace with humanity's essence. Bearing the Sovereign's seal, the heart unifies the spiritual and material worlds. Our inner and outer beauties are in fact different dimensions of the life of our heart, and the radiance of our appearance is intimately tied to our inner life. When a word is spoken from the heart, the mind is ignited and our consciousness glows like the corona of the sun. At this moment, when the spirit turns its face to the secret voice of the heart, our feelings begin to resonate as if plucked by a mysterious plectrum, and our conscience begins to whirl like a dervish in joy

---

[42] According to the Qur'an, Jesus revived the dead with his word or breath. (See Qur'an, 3:49)

[43] A reference to the Qur'anic concept of spiritual "trade" mentioned in the verse: *"Those who recite God's scripture, keep up the prayer, give secretly and openly from what We have provided for them, may hope for a trade that will never decline."* (35:29)

and respect. We feel love's fire on all sides, and tears of joy quench the suffering of our longing.

When we lose our self and our will in ecstasy, we may temporarily lose our balance. But the heart always remains humble in the presence of God. When we travel in the realm of the heart, we are neither perplexed nor inhibited. If the hero of the heart halts with fright or struggles in his way with difficulty, love succors him like Khidr, holding the reins of his horse and carrying him swiftly over the pits of hesitation.[44] Our senses, inner and outer, are soldiers at the heart's command; they are moths fluttering around its brilliant light. The heart speaks with the highest authority, and all our senses submit to its rule. Like the pole star, it orbits only itself, chanting the name of God, while all other senses turn around it, prostrate.

All of us are guests in the house of the heart. Let us sacrifice our hearts to the One whose sovereignty is felt in this house. We are determined to offer our souls to the Sovereign, and we await His judgment. Since the day He breathed life into our hearts, our longing for reunion has bound us to Him, and we have diligently tended to our love as to a great weaving. Our soul trembles with excitement when we feel the nearness of the Friend; we wait patiently for Him to open the door, our heads bowed in respect.

As we walk on this way, singing the ballads of longing and love, the heart is our gracious guide. Until our last breath, we promise to follow this blessed guide.

August 1990

---

[44] Khidr, the "Green One," is a spiritual personality and a man of wisdom in Islamic tradition, who lives in an angelic way, serving God by following divine commands. He is believed to succor people in hard conditions.

Love

The essence of every creature is love. Love is a brilliant light and the greatest power in the world; there is no enemy on earth that cannot be overcome by it. When love fills a soul, that soul is elevated and prepared for eternal life. It is love that inspires us to share the beauties of eternity with others, and we endure all sufferings for the sake of love. The soul that pronounces "love" with its last breath will be raised in the Hereafter by the breaths of love.

It is impossible for those souls that do not know love to flourish or rise to the heights of true humanity. Even if they were to live for hundreds of years, they could not advance toward maturity. Unable to escape from the dark labyrinths of the ego, such souls cannot love in true sense of the word. They cannot feel love, and they perish unaware of the love that lies at the heart of the universe.

We first encounter love as children, when we first open our eyes to the world and see our parents' faces, flushed with compassion. We grow up to trust the hearts that beat with love. In the course of our lives, we sometimes find this love and sometimes don't. But we are always chasing after it.

Love shines in the face of the sun; the waters evaporate and rise toward it. Once condensed, these drops descend to the bosom of the earth on wings of love. The flowers that receive this blessing bloom with love and offer their smiles to other lovers. On their leaves, the dew dances and twinkles with love. Lambs bleat and nuzzle with love, while the birds form choirs of love. Every creature participates in the grand orchestra of love, each taking its place in the brilliant symphony and giving voice to the deep love that rests in the bosom of the universe.

Love captivates the human soul so completely that many will leave their home for its sake, and many will leave their hearths ruined behind. In every valley, a Majnun groans with longing for a Layla.[45] But those with shallow hearts, who do not comprehend the love that moves in their own soul, dismiss this longing as madness.

It is right to live for the sake of others, and love is the origin of this virtue. The greatest heroes of humanity are those who participate in this altruistic love, uprooting all hatred from their soul. Death cannot still the breath of such heroes, and winter cannot cause their flowers to fade. In their inwardness, these gorgeous souls kindle a new torch of love with each new day. They make their hearts into gardens of kindness, and love forges the pathways between these gardens of kindness and the hearts of all others. They receive the privilege of eternal life from such a Supreme Authority that not even doomsday, let alone death, can destroy their harvest.

A mother who can die for the sake of her child is a heroine of compassion. A man who can sacrifice his life for the sake of his country is a champion of courage. One who lives and dies for the sake of humanity is a monument of immortality. In the hands of these heroes, love is a weapon strong enough to conquer every enemy and a key that will open every door. Those who possess it will ultimately be welcomed at every gate. Bearing love as a censer, they will spread the fragrance of peace to all corners of the earth.

The path of love is the quickest way to win the hearts of others; it is the path of the Prophets. Those who walk on it will not be rejected, for if one door is closed, thousands more will be opened. When we enter hearts by the path of love, no problem can remain unsolved.

Happy are those who follow the guidance of love! How unfortunate are those who do not know of the love in their soul and who live their entire life as if deaf and dumb!

O Lord! We take refuge in Your love on these days when hatred and enmity envelop everything in darkness. We come to Your door one more time, beseeching You to fill the hearts of Your wayward servants with love and virtue.

March 1987

---

[45] Layla and Majnun are legendary lovers in classical Islamic literature. Denoting the man, *"majnun"* literally means "madman," namely, one who has gone mad from love and longing.

Mercy

Mercy is the leaven of creation, its crucial ingredient. Through mercy, existence first came into harmony, and it is mercy that allows it to continue. Without mercy, all creation would be chaos.

The earth was set in order by the messages of mercy, revealed from beyond the heavens. Everything attained its proper balance in mercy. The harmonious operation of the universe is a rehearsal for eternal existence in the Hereafter, and every creature moves toward this end. As order is manifest in all movements, mercy gleams in all activity.

This all-encompassing mercy refuses to go unnoticed. It manifests itself in the wind and in the dancing of the waters. Clouds hover above our heads on the wings of mercy, and it is through mercy that rain comes to our aid. Lightning and thunder proclaim the good news of that secret mercy; all nature recites the praises of the Infinitely Merciful One. The land, sea, and vegetation all sing the songs of mercy and compassion in their own languages.

Consider the worm: Under our feet, it is greatly in need of our compassion. But at the same time, it is a diligent traveler that shows mercy to many things. It deposits hundreds of eggs in the soil that graciously enfolds it; thus, the soil is aerated and made propitious for vegetation. The earth and the worm show mercy to each other under our feet, but we ignore this fact and mercilessly abuse nature. Poor man! He is unaware of the injustice of his own actions.

Now look at that bee that visits thousands of flowers and the silkworm that confines itself to its cocoon. How much hardship they endure in order to join in this symphony of compassion! How can we not acknowledge what these self-sacrificial creatures suffer in order to feed us honey and clothe us in silk? Have you considered what a hero of compassion the chicken is when she sacrifices herself to save her young from a fox? Or the wolf that offers the food she finds to her young, forgetting her own hunger?

In nature, everything bears witness to compassion and radiates compassion. The universe performs a symphony of compassion: Different voices and tunes merge in rhythms so perfect that only an all-encompassing mercy could be directing this mysterious music. How unfortunate are those souls who understand nothing of this.

In the face of such compassion, it is our responsibility to comprehend this universal mercy and offer ourselves to it. As humans, we are obliged to show mercy to all humanity and to all of nature. The more we show mercy, the more we are elevated. But when we resort to injustice and wrongdoing, we disgrace ourselves and become a shame to humanity.

According to the Prophet, peace and blessings be upon him, a prostitute went to Paradise because she gave water to a miserable dog dying of thirst. Another woman went to Hell because she left her cat confined at home until it died of hunger. Be merciful so that you may receive mercy. When someone shows mercy once here on earth, they receive thousands of heavenly tidings in return. Our ancestors comprehended this truth and founded a great many homes of compassion everywhere. Their concern reached far beyond humanity, and they established foundations to protect and cherish animals as well, for mercy was their temperament. Some compassionate people were even inspired to establish a sanctuary for injured birds.[46]

Alas! I wish we would show as much mercy to people as our ancestors were ready to show to animals. But we have not even been compassionate to ourselves, and so we have taught new generations our merciless indifference. Indeed, it is we ourselves who made society uninhabitable with its myriad suffocating developments.[47]

---

[46] The author refers to some charitable initiatives in Ottoman Empire dedicated to caring for animals, such as the "Foundation for Poor Storks" in Bursa, established to care for migrating storks.

[47] This specifically refers to the severe social turmoil in Turkey during the year of publication of this article. In September 1980, a military coup occurred, allegedly to stop increasing violent struggles among different ideological groups in society.

We should point out, however, that the feeling of mercy may be abused. And the exploitation of mercy is as displeasing and harmful as the absence of mercy. Where mercy is aptly shown, it is like the water of life. But where misused, it becomes a poison. In this way, mercy is like water: Only if oxygen and hydrogen are joined in a proper ratio can they form the element most vital to life. Likewise, we must show mercy in the proper proportion and know who deserves it. Showing mercy to a monster only fuels its appetite. Granting compassion to atrocious individuals will only encourage them to be more aggressive. It is not fitting to show mercy to those who take pleasure in poisoning others. In doing so, we surrender the world to cobras. Mercy shown to the bloodthirsty is mercilessness to their victims; when we have mercy upon the wolf, we neglect the rights of the lamb. Such an attitude will undoubtedly please the wolves, but it will cause the rest of creation to cry with sorrow.

November 1980

Forgiveness and Tolerance

The human being is a creature in which many faults and many virtues co-inhere. No other creature is host to such contradictions. We are unusual, we who can simultaneously soar in the skies of paradise and fall into the pits of hell. And we search in vain for any correlation between our eminence and our misery. Causality follows a strange course in us, unlike any other in nature. Sometimes, we bend only to spring back like wheat in the wind; other times we fall like giant sycamores, never to rise again. Our actions can make even the angels envious, or we can be so vile that even the devils feel ashamed.

Because our nature is purely potential, error is inevitable. But this does not mean that error itself is a part of our essence. Errors may tarnish us and wrongs may spoil our initial purity, but these stains are only incidental. And so for humanity, forgiveness is everything.

To ask forgiveness and feel regret for a missed opportunity are matters of mindfulness and possess great worth. But it is more valuable to forgive, for this is a matter of dignity and virtue. Forgiveness is virtuous, and virtue requires forgiveness. The well-known proverb has much to say here: "Errors from the younger, forgiveness from the elder." To be forgiven is to be restored; forgiveness brings us back to our essence, where we find ourselves anew. Thus, the attitudes and actions that encourage such a quest for return are the most pleasing in the sight of the All-Merciful One.

Forgiveness was brought into creation with humanity. When God first made His forgiveness known to humanity, He placed the beauty of forgiveness in our heart. With the first mistake of Adam and Eve, humanity wronged itself. Then, when remorse flooded their conscience and they cried to the heavens, it was forgiveness that descended in response.[48] Throughout ages, we have cherished this precious inheritance as our hope and consolation. Whenever we err, we remember the sanctuary of that first forgiveness; thus, we shed our embarrassment and obtain the blessing of infinite mercy. Then we too are generous with forgiveness, laying it like a veil over the faults of others.

Thanks to the hope offered by forgiveness, we can rise above our limited horizon and see the world in its true light. The fortunate ones who are lifted up on the wings of forgiveness will feel relief in their spirit. Can we imagine a person who enjoys being forgiven but is deprived of the joy of forgiving? We love forgiving just as we love being forgiven. How can we not forgive, we who know that the waters of forgiveness will assuage the inner suffering of others? Especially once we have comprehended that to receive forgiveness, we must first practice the virtue of forgiving.

Those who forgive are honored with forgiveness in turn. But those who do not forgive will not be forgiven. Those who preclude tolerance from their hearts are utterly deprived of their humanity. Since they do not feel remorse over their own faults, they will not feel the lofty pleasure of forgiveness. When Jesus, peace be upon him, spoke to a crowd that was preparing to stone a sinner, he said: "Let the person among you who is without sin be the first to cast a stone at her."[49] If we have truly learned this touching lesson, how could we even consider punishing someone else? Do we not already deserve punishment ourselves? If only those who waste their life keeping a record of the faults of others would understand this! It is true that the guilty should be punished for justice, and compassion is not to interfere with such punishment. However, there is no justice in punishing those whom we have convicted in hatred and enmity. And unless we are ready to

---

[48] The Qur'an teaches that the first human error was Adam and Eve's mutual fault. But it was not an original or hereditary sin, for sin or crime is a personal matter. God forgave Adam and Eve upon their repentance, even though He drove them out of the Garden for the purpose of trial. (See Qur'an 2:35-39; 7:23-24)

[49] John 8:7.

destroy the idols of our ego as courageously as Abraham, peace be upon him, we will never be able to judge ourselves or others in truth.[50]

Forgiveness came to the world with humankind and reached its perfection with humankind. We witness the immense scope of forgiveness in the life of the Prophet, the most perfect man. As for hatred and enmity, they are the seeds of hell, spread by malignant souls. Against these advocates of animosity, who would turn the earth into an abyss, we must bring forgiveness to all those in crisis. Those who are strangers to forgiveness and tolerance have filled our recent history with pain. We cannot help but tremble when we consider that these same inauspicious ones might rule the future as well. Therefore, we must teach our children and our grandchildren the virtue of forgiveness, which persists even against the crudest behaviors and most unsettling events.

Nonetheless, it would be an insult to the very virtue of forgiveness if we were to show tolerance to the monsters of humanity. Such brutal souls enjoy the torture and suffering of others, and it is out of our respect for humanity that we cannot forgive them. Nobody can justify such forgiveness.

In our recent past, generations have been raised in the schools of hostility, and many have witnessed the horror of the battlefields into which they were thrown.[51] What could they learn from a society whose breath reeked of blood? Even the morning horizon appeared to be red with it. The cruel events of their time mocked the aspirations of their souls. If only we could recognize the suffering of these generations: They have been brutalized by false teachings for so many years that they know nothing but corruption and rebellion.

We believe that forgiveness and tolerance are heavenly cures that will heal our wounds if properly prescribed. But an incorrect application of forgiveness will create overwhelming new complications:

---

[50] The Qur'an narrates that Prophet Abraham smashed the idols of his polytheistic community in a brave manner. (21:57-58)

[51] This paragraph refers to the negative social and political context in Turkey during the decades preceding the article's publication.

First diagnose the illness, then set out the treatment.
Do you think that every ointment is a cure for every wound? [52]

March 1980

---

[52] Ziya Pasha (d. 1880), Turkish-Ottoman statesman, author, and poet.

Virtue and Happiness

Those who promise our people happiness must first equip them with virtue. For the hearts that are devoid of virtue, happiness is out of reach. Throughout history, sound minds have always agreed upon this: Felicity and virtue must exist together.

Put simply, virtue requires only morality and love. A virtuous person acknowledges his relationship with all creation and beholds all things in love. Life moves around him like a cool breeze and fills his heart with joy. He discerns the wisdom at work in the constant flow of events and is therefore always full of wonder and joy. Neither sunset nor nightfall can spoil his delight or inspire gloom in his heart. He lives in peace and bliss amidst creation's ever-renewed landscape.

Virtue does not demand the rejection of all human desire or an asceticism that renounces material things. Such practices would only isolate us from others and foster dissatisfaction with the world. This is the death of happiness, as Henrik Ibsen puts it. For once we have denied the world, we can only be concerned with ourselves and thus be deprived of the virtue of generosity. This sort of asceticism is a misunderstanding of morality, for true virtue lies in living for the sake of others.

On the other hand, it is wrong to claim that virtue guarantees material and spiritual felicity. A virtuous person can be ill, poor, and in a wretched state; he may face oppression, humiliation, or betrayal; he may suffer tortures, condemnations, or exile. Jesus was oppressed, Socrates was convicted, and Epictetus was banished. But these virtuous ones were happy despite their suffering, for happiness signifies the presence of an inner paradise grounded in pure faith. To borrow Nursi's words, faith contains the Tuba seed of Paradise, whereas unbelief contains the Zaqqum seed of Hell.[53]

Virtue requires that we humbly recognize our finitude within this boundless universe and not exaggerate our own merit. Otherwise, we are likely to become unhappy once our insatiable ambitions are disappointed and our pride is hurt. A virtuous man is a man of reason. He does not despair over problems that have a solution, nor does he wail over those that have none. He avoids hardship when he can but chooses to submit to the divine will in the face of events beyond his control. Life's unavoidable adversities do not surprise him and cannot spoil his joy, for he is already prepared to face them. His happiness is not compromised by egotism, base thoughts, or the desire for wealth and status. He is content with the pleasure he takes in the joys of love, compassion, and friendship.

As he refuses to indulge in feelings of betrayal, revenge, hatred, and jealousy, the breezes of love and respect comfort him and make him joyful. He will savor the spiritual pleasure that comes from sharing the joys of others, freeing them from their sufferings, and leading them to happiness. His concern for his family, his country, indeed for all of creation, is like an ocean without shore. In this way, he experiences the limitless pleasures of Paradise without leaving this world.

Virtue also joins us to the past and the future and brings us into spiritual community with the many virtuous people who have come before us and who will succeed us. And through virtuous deeds, we seek their approval and appreciation. In other words, to be virtuous is to share in the lives of both our ancestors and our children. When our hearts dwell in this intimate relationship with all humanity, external conditions can no longer disturb our happiness. We thus attain eternal bliss in this world.

This deep relationship between virtue and true happiness has been revealed to us by the noblest teachers. This is the kind of happiness in which hearts are satisfied and minds are given confidence. This

---

[53] In Islamic sources, Tuba is a glorious tree in Paradise with pleasant fruits, in contrast to the Zaqqum tree in Hell with its terrible taste. (See Qur'an 37:62)

happiness is rooted in the strongest principles of virtue: maturity, humility, forgiveness, and tolerance. It is a spiritual happiness, so central to our essence that nothing else can replace it. Material happiness can contribute nothing to it, nor can it distract us from our spiritual joy. How happy are those who elevate their soul in faith and adorn their heart with virtues!

June 1982

Inner Peace

For as long as humanity has existed, we have dreamed of peace, obsessed over it, chased after it, and struggled for its sake. We have sought peace through hard work and material prosperity, through the fulfillment of desire in unlimited freedom, through technological advancements that promote physical comfort, and through the pleasure and gratification of sexual desire. In these ways, humanity has dedicated its life to the attainment of peace. But even though we have plenty of reasons to be hopeful, we never reach our destination. How could we? The peace that we pursue is the fruit of true virtue and can only be attained through the merit of perfect faith. This is the essence of the call of the Prophets.

If we want to attain peace, we must turn to God and submit our whole existence to Him. A believer living in such complete submission cannot be a captive to his carnal desires, nor will he fear anything but God. When he enters the protection of his Beloved, the Almighty, he is at peace at last. He knows that God, with absolute power and grace, will never forsake those who turn to Him and never let them fall into misery.

For this reason, it is the believer who can truly feel the breezes of peace and security, and he will achieve this goal if he commits his life totally to God. He will be protected in his path and reunited with God in the realms beyond. His faith gives him confidence, his submission strengthens his conscience, and he entrusts his willpower to the divine authority. Thus, he passes over every snare of sensuality and overcomes the urge of animal desires. With the Qur'an as his guide, he advances toward the purpose of his existence. Indeed, those who take shelter in the Qur'an's guidance will feel in their soul a deep contentment and an unshakable trust; they will breathe with confidence and security. As they contemplate life and reflect upon eternity, a growing awareness of their exceptional responsibility will fill them with hope. This hope is directly proportional to the depth of their faith. Such believers consider everything from the perspective of divine mercy. If the curtain of material appearances were removed, they would see the eternal reality smiling at their good fortune.

Faith is the key to happiness in this life and the next. It promises a pleasant rest after death to all who take refuge in it. Faith offers us the glad tidings of a gentle resurrection and merciful judgment. It unlocks the unimaginable treasures of Paradise, where we will at last witness God's infinite beauty and partake in His eternal pleasure. The promises of faith can sustain us through even the most difficult trials.

When we as believers turn our whole existence toward God, everything else fades from our sight. The forces and powers of falsehood deflate like balloons. The glow of this transient world, which can dazzle our eyes with its glitter, grows faint in the light that He shines into our heart. We begin to hear everywhere the proclamation: "Today all sovereignty belongs to God, the One, the All-Powerful."[54] At this point, our hearts are freed from the deceptive promises of false powers, false mercies, and false graces. We turn to Him alone for help. When our hearts are shaken with adversities, we trust in and rely solely on Him. In the sanctuary of His merciful providence, which encompasses all existence, we are guarded against all threats. When we are weak, we are protected by His transcendent power. When tainted by sin, we are bathed in the basin of His forgiveness. Through our faith, reliance, and submission to Him, we disperse the fog that obscures our horizon. Thus we face the future without surrender. We approach our individual, familial, and social problems with a conscience that is rooted in Him. There is no loneliness that we cannot overcome. Although we may experience temporary exile, our faith and submission always ground us in what is familiar. We welcome with patience and trust whatever difficulty befalls us.

As believers, our faith and wisdom have made us acquaintances with everything. We engage with all creatures as friends. We are involved

---

[54] A paraphrase of a Qur'anic verse about the Day of Judgment (Qur'an, 40:16).

in the world, and take the honor of our "vicegerency" seriously. Aware that all things have been created for our sake, we bow before God in gratitude and humility. Our souls are in the company of the angels, indeed of the entire universe. Nature stands before us as our ancestral home, and the world welcomes us like a mother's bosom. We pay no heed to the teachings of materialism or naturalism, and we relate everything in the universe to God. Thus we are welcomed by everything in response. We are secure in all things, and we offer security to all. We are not scared of anyone, and we do not frighten anyone. Instead, we embrace all of humanity, our brothers and sisters, and smile at all creatures. We taste and enjoy all of God's gifts: the water and the air, the soil and the flowers, the gardens and the mountains. We greet the whole world with the language of the heart and show affection to its creatures, our companions and fellow guests. In all our actions, we demonstrate our purpose: to call creation to agreement and reconciliation.

Through faith, the believer finally achieves the peace that humanity longs for. In enviable calm, he is enraptured by faith's indescribable pleasures. A stranger to aggression and dispute, he only uses his strength to share his delights with others, revealing to them new horizons of possibility. He always endeavors to help others live, placing their needs before his own. He trusts God infinitely and never turns against people. His strength may come from God's absolute power, but he does not despise the assistance of other believers. Forces that would oppose him are transmuted by the depth of his faith into trials that strengthen him; thus, he advances toward his purpose unfazed. Through faith and service to others, he enjoys the peace and pleasure of God.

Society will only be ready for peace when its individuals have reached such a state of contentment, loving and respecting each other from their hearts. Then, the causes of disharmony will fade away. Individuals will not be divided by the distinctions and privileges of nobility or neighborhood. Once everyone and everything is acknowledged to be under the authority of the Absolute Origin, then we will truly become brothers and sisters, as the Qur'an teaches.[55] This rela-

---

[55] Qur'an, 49:10.

tionship is not superficial: Love and compassion will hold us together like the organs of a single body, to use the words of the Prophet. Then we will become each other's eyes and ears, tongue and lips, hands and feet, sharing each other's pains and feeling each other's joys.

In such a society, individuals commit their lives to the happiness of others, and there is no loneliness or misery among them. Children revere their parents like saints, and parents raise their children with diligent care. Spouses always treat each other with joy, for when they consider their eternal togetherness in the Hereafter, even old age is like an early romance. Their shared life traces to path of conscience and reason, and they move beyond the fickle swinging of emotion. They are so loyal to each other that not even dreams or thoughts could distract them from their love.

A nation can also become like this family of peace, existing in perfect harmony. In a nation composed of such families, people will treat each other with compassion and respect. They will wish to see their neighbors succeed and work to eliminate evils. They think well of everyone, are not wary of anyone, and do not denigrate anyone's honor. In such a nation, people are not pursued or arrested on mere suspicion. One part of society does not dedicate its life to the destruction of another. People do not resort to conspiracy, mendacity, and slander.[56] In this society of conscience and peace, people are in a constant battle against evils, for they have pledged to protect human virtue.

February 2000

---

[56] These sentences are particularly associated with the chaotic and uneasy social and political atmosphere in Turkey following the "postmodern" military coup in February 1997.

A Portrait of the Man of the Heart

The man of the heart is a hero of faith, action, and vision. His depth is not measured by his knowledge, but by the richness of his heart, the purity of his soul, and his closeness to God. For him, scientific achievements are valuable only insofar as they point toward the truth. Whatever does not help to reveal the reality of the universe, whatever knowledge has no practical benefit, is of no importance to him.

The person of the heart is dedicated to his spiritual life. He is determined to keep far away from all material and spiritual imperfection. He guards himself vigilantly against the corporeal desires; he vigorously struggles against hatred, animosity, greed, jealousy, selfishness, and lust. He is a monument of modesty and humility, and he always seeks the truth. He is quick to communicate what he knows about the world, yet is patient and prudent. Rather than proclaim his own ideas loudly, he puts them into practice, making himself an example to others. He hastens to his purpose, which is to aid others in their approach to God. His heart burns like a furnace with compassion for his people. But he never reveals his suffering; he only offers his warmth to all souls who will take refuge in him.

The man of the heart always fixes his sight on the realms beyond. He is tirelessly devoted to God's pleasure, running like a noble steed toward his goal. He runs, expecting nothing in return. Such a sincere disciple of the truth is ready to give up all everything for its sake. He opens his heart to everyone and embraces all people with compassion. He stands in the midst of the community like a protective angel, not expecting anything from anyone but God. He seeks harmony with all and does not harbor hostility toward anyone. Although he nourishes his own understanding, he does not enter into rivalry with others. Instead, he loves all who serve society and help revive the religious and moral virtues. He applauds their actions appreciatively and respects their understanding where it differs from his own.

The man of the heart depends ultimately on God's providence; nevertheless, he does not neglect his own endeavors. In all his actions, he seeks God's grace. He takes pains to promote unity among the community, for the Qur'an considers solidarity to be an important vessel of the divine grace. He is willing to compromise his own opinions, seeking cooperation with all who walk on right paths. For blessing comes in unity, and discord and conflict lead nowhere.

The man of the heart is a lover of God and a devotee of His pleasure. No matter where he is or what his circumstances, he subordinates all his actions to God's consent. In his ambition to please God, he will give away everything he possesses in this world and the next. There is no room in his language for such false phrases as "my success" or "my achievement." No matter who has fulfilled a task, he rejoices as if the achievement had been his own. He respects the achievements of others and willingly leaves the honor of leadership to others. For in his humility, he assumes others to be more successful and more capable of service. He prepares for others a place in which they can serve and then retreats from public view, easily mistaken for an ordinary person among many others.

The man of the heart always questions himself. He is so busy with his own failings that he has no time to criticize the faults of others. He does his best to exemplify goodness and to direct the gaze of others toward God. He turns a blind eye to the faults of others, responding to their mistreatment with a smile. In this way, he overcomes their misdeeds with kindness. He never intends to offend anyone, no matter how many times he is hurt. He does not violate the rights of any person or respond to an attack with anger. He acts calmly even in the most urgent situations. Regardless of his circumstances, he is always preoccupied with his spiritual task, striving to live according to his heart.

The man of the heart must dedicate his life to God in perfect faith; this is his first priority. He will have so devoted his feelings, thoughts, and actions to God's pleasure that not even Paradise can distract him from his purpose. He does not compete with those who share this purpose, nor is he jealous of them. On the contrary, he compliments them where they are weak. He knows that all believers are like organs of the same body. In a spirit of perfect altruism, he chooses to reward his companions with position, fame, and influence instead of himself. Stepping into the background, the man of the heart proclaims the successes of others, applauds their achievements, and welcomes their attainments with joy.

Although the man of the heart follows his own path and acts according to his own character, he is respectful of the ideas and contributions of others. He is ready to share and live together with the community. He collaborates with those who share his ideals, working with them to establish an "us" in place of every "me." Moreover, he readily sacrifices his own felicity for the happiness of others. But he does not expect any praise for his renunciation, for that would discredit his sincerity. He flees the limelight and runs from fame as if they were wild beasts; his wish is to be completely forgotten.

The man of the heart lives according to the guidance of the Qur'an and the Prophet: sincerely pious, a friend of God, and constantly aware of His presence. He is vigilant against egotism, arrogance, and pride. When good things are attributed to him, he reminds others of their true Owner, saying simply: "All is from Him." Concerning the matters of human will, he escapes the limitations of "me" and takes refuge in "us." He does not fear anybody, and he does not know panic. He "relies upon God, holds fast to his efforts, and submits to God's providence."[57] He does not hesitate to work for what he knows is right.

The man of the heart does not resent anyone, especially those who are also committed to God. If he sees any of his companions doing something wrong, he does not abandon them or embarrass them in any way. He only reproaches himself for seeing the wrong; he only questions himself. At all costs, he avoids thinking badly of believers and is always quick to give them the benefit of the doubt.

The man of the heart acts in the confidence that this world is a place of service, not a place of reward. Even as he performs his duties

---

[57] A quotation from a poem by Mehmed Akif.

with exceptional discipline, he considers it disrespectful to worry over their results, for it is God who determines everything. He recognizes that service to humanity, service to faith, and service to religion are the greatest tasks we can perform as we continue on the way toward God's pleasure. Yet however great his achievements may be, he never expects to benefit from them, either materially or spiritually.

The man of the heart does not fall into despair when his achievements are taken from him, nor is he shaken when people oppose him. He views this world as one of endurance, not one of resentment. Even while he bears his hardships in patience, he is always searching for new solutions and strategies.

To conclude, I would like to reiterate that today, when the human virtues are greeted with disdain, when religious thought is fractured, and when the noise of aimless people fills the air, such people of the heart are as necessary to survival as air and water.

August 2000

CHAPTER FOUR

EDUCATION

The Youth

Yours alone is this reform, this revolution.
Does not everything belong to you, Oh youth?[58]

The most important issues of our time concern the young generation. How do we give them what they are due and ask of them what we need? It is essential that we take seriously both the promises and the challenges of the coming generation.

The youth give shape to every change; they bring forth new eras. The Roman revolution was theirs, and Hellenism was theirs. The earth awaits the honor of their footsteps again, and the heavens listen for their voices. The seven wonders of the world are pillars to youth's magnificence. Their arching brows are crescent moons, and their smiles are as bright and mysterious as stars. Do not think I exaggerate: Even a thousand eulogies could not describe the glory of these young generations. Baqi says:

> *The breezes of spring blew like the breath of Jesus,*
> *And the flowers opened their eyes from the sleep of nonexistence.*[59]

If that magnificent poet of the Ottoman Empire had turned his gaze toward the youth—those who bring new life to us—he would similarly praise them.

Yet the ignorant consider the youth to be useless vagrants, and the advocates of anarchy enlist them as elements of destruction. But for us, the young generation represents incomprehensible potential. It is their nature to be lively and restless. If neglected, they will become a deadly poison. But when the young are rightly educated, their nobility is unsurpassed. Like heroes, they can overcome perils by the thou-

---

[58] Tevfik Fikret (d. 1915), Turkish-Ottoman poet.
[59] Baqi (d. 1600), Turkish-Ottoman poet.

sands. But they can also be made captives at the hands of lust. Everyone tries to lure the youth; everyone wants to obtain them. If you win their confidence, they will offer you relief and comfort. But if you don't hold them fast, they are easily carried off. If you offer them only vague ideals, any daydreamer can lead them astray. If you fix their minds on concrete things, they will become fetishistic. If you can free them from animal desires, they will acquire a second nature, but if you let them loose in the field of pleasures, they will crumble like a burned coal into nothing.

If you attend to them, the youth will rise to the summits, reciting:

> *When you imbibe that wine of divine love,*
> *The light of the universe shines into your heart and gives you eternal life.*[60]

But if you abandon them, they will fall into ruin, chanting:

> *Drink the wine and love the beautiful, if you are wise.*
> *Do not care whether the world exists or not.*[61]

The youth are pure potential. We must not neglect them, for they have not yet realized their nature. How can we neglect them? In our recent history, custody of the young was given to chauvinistic thinking.[62] Later, in a period of a total alienation, they were an unprecedented disaster: spoiled and unchaste. And today, the young generation groans like a painful ulcer in the stomach or a cataract in the eye. Their humanity is a fraud, their mercy is feigned, they spend themselves in deception, and their courage is an illusion. They are now disfigured, among the lowest of the low. However, the hand of a true educator can still shape them; they can still achieve the high stature that the universe has reserved for them. It is not too late for today's youth to receive the divine favor.

They long for a teacher, who will lead them from the rank of novice to the heights of mastery. Then, they will understand what harm

---

[60] Gedai (d. 1889), Turkish-Ottoman folk poet.

[61] Ziya Pasha (d. 1880).

[62] The author refers to the strict nationalism, enforced by the government in the early decades of the Turkish Republic.

the ignorant have done to them, and they will keep their distance from such empty lives. They expect protection and discernment from those who have gone before them, and we expect them to bring unity to their hearts and minds and embrace their virtuous history. They wait for a skilled doctor, who can cure the sickness that has gripped their souls and provide a remedy for the delusions that have grown old in their minds. They cry out, "Fire! Come to my help!" And we say, "Allow us to put out this fire with our sweat."

Oh, the community of mercy![63] If you cannot wait for the Day of Resurrection, then stand up! As Heracles rescued Prometheus, run to the help of our youth, who suffer now under the illusions of their own desires.

August 1977

---

[63] Originally: *ümmet-i merhume*, a classical Turkish phrase to refer to the entire Muslim community. The phrase literally means: "the community upon which God has mercy."

Elevating Humanity

Your essence is even loftier than angels.
Realms are hidden in you, worlds compacted.[64]

Humanity is essentially the subject of every philosophical and scientific theory. No philosophy can be articulated, or any science developed, without first taking human beings into consideration. All study is an attempt to understand humanity in both its physical and metaphysical dimensions, for all other things have significance and value only in relation to humanity. All branches of the sciences gather around us to discuss our various aspects. Books hasten to us, fill themselves with us, and thus become radiant.

Human beings are so perfectly tuned, our biological functions so perfectly adjusted, that we manifest the ideal structure. We cannot help but admire the anatomy of our every organ, not to mention the eternally unfolding depths of our spiritual nature. An intricate brain and an ineffable spirit held together in perfect harmony! Every aspect of the human being is like a magnificent work of art, worthy of wonder. But here we will not deal with humanity's marvelous appearance or the inward dimensions beyond it, but on our unique potential and ability.

The human being in all his aspects is a difficult creature to understand. His peculiarities begin when he first enters the world. Other creatures possess perfect instincts and knowledge of the laws of life; they come into the world as if they had already been trained in another one. But the human being, the most magnificent and esteemed of all creatures, emerges without any knowledge and with none of the skills necessary for life. Beyond the mechanical order of his body, everything in him develops according to his reason, will, freedom, and introspec-

---

[64] Mehmed Akif (d. 1936).

tion. In this way, his inner and outer existences are integrated, and he becomes a self. This capacity for synthesis is the greatness of humanity, but it can only be developed through education. If we were to simply leave humanity to its instincts, unable to realize the potential of its identity, this would be like leaving a seed without soil.

The lion is equipped with its paw and the bull with its horns, but humanity must prepare all means of survival for itself. We must use our intellect, will, and reason to invent what is beneficial and prevent what is harmful. In this way, we build a civilization in which we can find peace as individuals. Then future generations will inherit the works and virtues cultivated by the hearts and minds of all humanity. This is natural, for the human being is not concerned with the present alone. The past and the future are also present in his mind and essential to his existence. This is why the many contributors to the development of science and philosophy did not quit working, even when they knew they would not enjoy the fruits of their labor. They worked in the name of knowledge and culture for all humanity and left an astounding heritage behind them. Without such selflessness, there can be no civilization on earth.

But the efforts of past generations have given us more than just material development; they have also left us with a heritage of virtue. It is according to the wisdom of those who have gone before us that we develop our capabilities, plan our behaviors, and channel our efforts to good purpose. Throughout history, generations have always set themselves the task of educating subsequent generations, for education is the greatest gift they have to offer. Education fixes humanity's attention on lofty purposes and keeps us from the distraction of our animal inclinations. By providing a frame and context for our activities, education keeps us from wild degeneration. Through education, our capabilities are allowed to flourish, and we unearth the potential hidden in our soul.

In the heart of humanity, there are only seeds of goodness; therefore, even feelings like lust and anger can lead indirectly to beautiful outcomes. Through education, this becomes possible. In other words, only after our capacity for reason, will, and introspection are brought to fruition by education can we become truly human. Then we transcend our animal existence, achieve autonomy in nature, and bind ourselves to the Being of absolute independence.

Human reason, as defined by philosophy, is our ability to draw conclusions from given premises. This intellectual activity distinguishes us from the rest of creation. Reason is a special endowment to humanity, but we do not receive it in its mature form. It is ours only as a potential that we must develop. When reason is united with conscience, it gains a new identity as the link between our inner and outer existences. Then, our conscience guides our behavior. In this sense, the ultimate purpose and highest ideal of human reason is the attainment of the knowledge of God. With this knowledge, reason reaches maturity and perfection, and we come to know our moral responsibilities.

Freedom is a consequence of the autonomy we enjoy as humans. We have free control over our actions, but we are also uniquely accountable for them. One should reject the materialist understanding in which humanity's actions are fully determined like the movements of a machine, for it is impossible to discuss morality without first positing freedom. As moral creatures, we possess a dimension that is not determined by the laws of nature: Our conscience clearly signifies the existence of a transcendent realm, to which we are bound by our responsibility to differentiate right from wrong.

When we reflect upon the external world in our conscience, we catch a glimpse of what is beyond this realm of contingency. In contemplation, we are elevated beyond our spatial limitations. The degree of such "ascension" depends on the quality of our intellectual activity, the determination of our will, and the depth of our introspection. Every individual is capable of contemplation, and each of us can share in it according to our abilities. Ascension brings us to the ultimate attainment of the inner life: contemplation of the Creator's unique beauty.

For centuries, our people have neglected this lofty journey. But it is our duty, particularly as educators, to help the younger generations attain the knowledge of their human essence. We must nurture their reason and vitalize their will. We must help them purify their feelings and connect with what is beyond nature. If we do not raise the young to the dignity of their human potential, history will hold us responsible for their total alienation.

July 1979

Our Philosophy of Education (I)

The beginning of a new school year is a prudent time for us to re-examine our system of education. For a school is a vital laboratory of the future, its courses are the potions of life, and its teachers are the heroic masters of healing.

School is where we are taught everything about life and what lies beyond it. Of course, life itself is a place of learning, but it is only through school that we are introduced to this fullness of life. Education focuses the light of wisdom on life's events so that students can comprehend their environment. It illuminates the meaning of phenomena and brings integrity to our thoughts. Education gives our contemplation consistency and unifies creation's multiplicity. In this sense, a school is no different than a sanctuary, with the teachers its revered saints.

A good school is like a pavilion full of angels: It develops individual virtues and guides its students toward the dignity of their spirit. At a good school, children learn the mysteries of the self and realize their potential. But if pupils are imbued with vulgarity and alienated from each other, a school is nothing but a ruin. For some centuries now, such twisted institutions have been a cause for our embarrassment.

The true teacher sows and cultivates the seeds of virtue. He is attentive to that which is good and wholesome. He sets goals for the students and offers them direction in the face of life's vicissitudes. It is in school that life's abundant flow acquires a distinct identity. In other words, like a confluence of rivers, a school consolidates the plurality of life into a whole. It is in school that we train our minds to bring unity to the dispersion of life's events.

It would be a mistake to assume that school is only relevant during certain periods of life. On the contrary, school introduces students to a lifetime of study. In this respect, our education influences every part of our lives, even if we never spent much time in a classroom. When pupils learn the lessons concerning truth, they will spend their entire lives reviewing them. What is of importance is that we utilize such lessons as guides on our way to virtue.

At school, knowledge is internalized in the form of wisdom. This allows us to transcend the material dimension and touch the boundaries of infinity. Knowledge that is not internalized is an embarrassing burden loaded on our shoulders. It is like a mischievous devil that causes confusion. Indeed, rote learning that does not illuminate the mind or elevate the soul will only erode our conscience and weary our heart.

The best form of knowledge that a school can provide is one that imbues the phenomena of the external world with the wisdom of the inner world. A good teacher can transform what appear to be external phenomena into integral parts of our inner life. Undoubtedly, life itself is the greatest guide and the truest master, continually repeating its lessons. However, we need practice before we can enroll in these illustrious lessons, and this practice is what our teachers offer. They mediate between our life and our conscience, teaching us to interpret the subtle language of phenomena.

Books, newspapers, radio and TV can teach us some things, but they can never teach us the reality of life or its presence within us. In this respect, a good teacher is irreplaceable. Every day, he or she manages to bring new passion into our hearts and leave indelible impressions on our minds. There are many things that students can be taught easily with the aid of technology, but the crucial lessons address the purpose of knowledge and require the presence of qualified teachers, who bring their lessons forth from the prisms of their hearts. This is the secret of the many great teachers in human history.

A good lesson is one that is learned in the presence of such a teacher. The students not only enrich their knowledge; they are also brought to the threshold of infinite unknown realities, to the point of enlightenment. Through our lessons, we begin to grasp the natural world as a lace curtain through which we contemplate eternal truths, or as a veil laid over the realms of mystery. In such a school, no one can ever get enough of learning. For teachers enjoy leading their pupils to the stars and bringing them to rest in their consciences. This is a kind of education that carries both students and teachers beyond the dimensions of their usual life.

Here is what we consider a true teacher to be: one who grasps the significance of phenomena and builds associations between life and conscience. The teacher hears the truth in everything and can express it in any language. School is like a laboratory for future generations, and the teacher is its physician. The teacher is the one who can heal our social ailments and remove the dark clouds from our horizon.

October 1979

Our Philosophy of Education (II)

Learning and teaching are two of humanity's lofty duties. The merits of education unearth our soul's capacities and fashion us into models of civility. Virtues cannot develop in individuals who have not been purified by education, nor is it useful to look to them for social loyalty.

But this raises important questions: What should we learn and what should we not learn? What should we teach and when should we teach it? Knowledge that is offered at the wrong time is like a fog that shrouds the mind. This kind of knowledge does not give light to its possessor and hence cannot benefit others. Although knowledge is valuable in itself, many times it can become a burden. To desire to know everything, or to seek knowledge for its own sake, leaves us with nothing but a barrage of mere information.

Education should help students integrate their personalities and discover the relationship between the external world and their inward experience. All knowledge should provide us with a sound basis for action and guide us to new syntheses. The kind of knowledge that does not address the mysterious relationship between humanity and nature will not contribute to our true understanding of existence or encourage our integration with it. Science of this kind only condemns our conscience with riddles. But the harmony between the perception and interpretation of the natural world gives conscience the freedom to fulfill its purpose.

It is dangerous to desire to know everything, given that some knowledge leads to harmful consequences. Instead of striving to become information addicts, we should direct our passion toward knowledge that facilitates our integration with the universe. This attitude is the origin of genuine thinking and the clearest sign that the true spirit of learning is present in us. To approach education in this spirit is to reject rote learning and mindless memorization. Then, we will not be deceived by mere appearances or mistake the peel of existence for the fruit.

Curiosity in everything, the indiscriminate desire for knowledge, is an obstacle to serious study. True thought only engages what is necessary. The things we learn needlessly, out of idle curiosity, can be harmful to our mind and heart, and especially harmful to the pure souls of youth.

When teaching the youth, we should help them see the meaning beyond appearances. In this practice, their age and sophistication should be taken into account, for children should not be given more than they can digest. In elementary school, for instance, children should not be put under the burden of the complicated subjects of world geography, human history, or philosophy. This would only instill in them doubts and hesitations.

It is impossible to comprehend the totality of our time: the infinite unfolding of events, the countless subjects of study, and the constant developments of research. Any attempt at such comprehension is clearly futile. Our time requires the division of labor, distribution of duties, and specialization. Students should devote themselves to a small part of the field of knowledge and seek to fulfill their role as students within that specialty.

Today, the family and social environment fail to motivate youth toward these educational ideals; the nobility of their inwardness is neglected. Their souls learn only the deadly lessons of their environment. In this context, they are not likely to preserve their original purity. The trifles of daily news, the endless games of political polemics, entertainment predicated on lies, deception, and sensation completely occupy their young minds. Even the heroes of spirituality could not endure such a burden! It is only natural, given the nature of these distractions, that youth struggle to understand the lessons of school, integrate them into their life, and achieve wisdom.

Today's students have been made lazy by a corrupt culture, and they pursue only what can be had with little effort. Pop culture preoccupies them with worthless goals and exploits their youthful fancies. In this context, it is incredibly difficult to teach them what it means to truly accomplish greatness. They find labor and exertion displeasing and will not endure systematic study. How can we cultivate virtue in youth whose minds are plagued daily by trivialities and whose hearts are wasted in meaningless struggles? If their animal instincts and lustful desires are encouraged every day, how will they find the strength to read and reflect?

The knowledge of goodness resists corruption and degeneration. The youth will receive this power first from the school of their teachers, then from the greater school of life. Only when they are equipped with this transcendent knowledge will they gain the strength to resist evils and rise on the wings of their will. On the other hand, the lack of this knowledge will leave the youth impotent and defenseless, and the knowledge of evil will paralyze them.

It is sad that more people do not take a stand against this social crisis or mobilize their resources to overcome it.

November 1979

What Education Promises

The happiness of a nation can only be sustained if new generations are raised up in the integrity of both heart and mind. But the youth of our time have been born into inauspicious bosoms of neglect. They find themselves in the midst of ruthless leaders, deadly ideologues, and debilitating media. It is our responsibility to rescue youth from this suffocating atmosphere, for it is their dynamic potential that will create for us a future. We must teach them how to exist by their own will: This is the sacred mission of all authorities and administrators.

We entrust our future to the youth. If they cannot acquire discernment through education, they will be crushed under the weight of base instincts and bad habits. Lust, rage, and greed will separate them from the essence of their humanity and enslave them to false convictions. According to modern pedagogy, such feelings can exert a powerful influence, even on the most educated youth, forcing them into error.

In reality, our human desires have been given to us because they can be enlisted in the service of good. Education teaches us to manage these feelings: We are fortified against their negative influences and able to direct them toward proper ends. Education teaches us how to employ even apparently harmful human emotions toward the goal of perfection. It enables the individual to develop the sense of virtue, the strength of will, the capacity for reflection, and the love of freedom that is service to the Truth.

The young generations suffer in the clutches of desire and ambition. If we fail to provide them with an education that addresses their true inwardness, if we fail to reveal to them the ways of morality and virtue, our nation will not escape its present turmoil. Obviously, nations that have successfully imparted to their young the nobility of ethics and culture will find in the new generation the guardians of sacred values; thus, their future is secure. But when nations neglect the moral and intellectual education of their children, they abandon their society to decadence and chaos.

Education should be among the primary concerns of nations, since it is so closely related to their vitality and longevity. It is even more important for a nation facing social and economic depression. In such a time of crisis, a society will be ruined if it does not diagnose its own predicament with clear eyes. If the nation obeys emotion rather than reason, if it gives in to despair or loses its way in the turbulence of the crowds, it will falter. Even the slightest errors in the matter of national education can result in enormous destruction. For all social crises, which scatter the individuals like the autumn leaves, could be said to originate in the lack of education and culture. If our national leaders cannot understand the significance of education and address instead thousands of inessential problems, then we must ask God for more patience as we wait for our Heracles.[65]

Today, we face a challenge more serious and more delicate than any other. We must teach our spiritual heritage to new generations and rescue them from alienation. Our efforts in the name of education will result in our future security and happiness, whereas our negligence and indifference will culminate in misery. Therefore, as responsible people, we must review the causes of our current social disorder and develop an objective plan for enlightening our children. This is the only way to save our country and nation.

We must raise generations who comprehend their time, who are able to consider the past, present, and future together. Otherwise, God forbid, our nation will be crushed in the merciless gears of history. Just as species become extinct when they fail to adapt to their environment, nations also pass away when they do not respond to the demands of their age. They surrender the field to other, more capable nations.

---

[65] Heracles is an image in Gülen's writings. Adopting from the Greek mythology, Gülen uses this image to refer to the heroic altruism of his ideal person of service.

The ruins of past civilizations and the fossils of extinct creatures both illustrate this divine principle.

The Egyptian civilization, the Roman Empire, the Andalusian culture, the Ottoman Empire: all were crushed by the same grim reality. They survive only as withered traces or ethnographic relics! The same fate awaits every nation that does not encourage its young to cultivate in themselves systematic thinking, willpower, and the love of God. These ideals will preserve them from indolence, discouragement, and panic, will inspire them to work with enthusiasm, and will evoke in them a public spirit.

Today we have to rethink our system of education in response to the social context of our time. We need to chart a new course from the past to present and from present to future, developing clear educational guidelines for new generations. In this regard, public authorities have a special responsibility. Until the day that vigorous minds and passionate hearts face up to this problem, how can we have confidence in the future of our country, or expect our nation to be elevated?

March 1984

What to Expect from Education

How should we raise up the new generations? What should we teach them, and why? And who is to fulfill this sacred duty? If we are to deal with the challenges of education, we must find persuasive answers to these questions. For a system of education without a clearly defined purpose will only confuse its students. Without method, teachers can only turn their students into empty vessels of information.

A nation's social structure is intimately related to its educational system: Society takes shape according to the education of its individuals. There is more than just the immediate future at stake, for the generations we raise today are likely to raise their children according to the same method. Just as marriage and reproduction are critical for a nation's physical existence, education is vital to its spiritual and moral existence. If the nation does not secure the institution of marriage, it cannot hope to survive. Likewise, unless nations give due importance to the spiritual and moral education of society, they will not escape downfall.

In a society, individuals influence the culture, and the culture plays an important role in shaping the individual. As the head of a family exerts great influence over its members, so too does the leader of a nation over its citizens. The elevation of a nation depends on the intellectual and spiritual culture that exists among its individuals and on the insightful and truthful service of the governing body. While administrators should work sincerely for the good of the public, the latter are also expected to endeavor to attain a role within society. This reciprocity reflects the Prophetic teaching: "All of you are shepherds, and all of you are responsible for those under your care." It also complies with the high ethical preference for social prosperity over personal prosperity.

Anyone involved in raising the younger generations, no matter their title, should not forget the responsibility that comes with this great task. As parents, we do our best to ensure a future for our children. We confront troubles and endure hardships so they can prosper. We work hard to prepare a paradise-like world for them. But if we fail to offer them the true prosperity of morality and virtue, will our effort not be wasted? A nation's greatest wealth is its culture of morality and virtue, and this capital accumulates only in the bosom of education. If a nation obtains this wealth, it will possess the power to conquer worlds and the key to the treasures of the universe. On the other hand, those masses deprived of it will lose their resources and be eliminated in life's struggle.

If we succeed in adorning the minds of the youth with the sciences of their time and instilling in their hearts the divine virtues, if we can teach them to view the future through the prism of history, our efforts will not have been in vain. Instead, we will reap much in return: Every penny spent on education of the youth will return to us as the wealth of cultured souls. As a nation, these will be our interminable treasures. For the well-educated generations will surmount all obstacles, will overcome all difficulties, whether material or spiritual, and will never fall into despair. They will not squander their spiritual inheritance; they will not know emptiness, hesitancy, or pessimism; they will not know misery.

Today, we are at a crossroads. We can either elevate our children to the truth of their humanity or abandon them to alienation. With this heavy responsibility on our shoulders, we must develop a program to reverse the decay brought about by past neglect. Otherwise, as the most precious gems of their existence begin to erode, the youth will lose sight of life's true value. They will cease to exist in their own distinct essence and will not be able to return to the glory of their past.

April 1984

CHAPTER FIVE

PEOPLE OF SERVICE

The People We Are Longing For

*"If I see the faith of my people secure,
I will be ready to be burned in Hell-fire.
For my heart would rejoice in a rose garden,
even if my body is in agony."*[66]

For many years, our nation has longed for liberators who will treat our wounds and cure us of our afflictions. Especially today, when the sky is dark and our paths multiply in confusion, we cling to this hope as if it were the water of life. Even when we begin to doubt that they will ever come, we never stop asking about them and singing ballads for their arrival.

Diogenes, overcome with pessimism, proclaimed the loss of humanity in his society. I wonder if we are able to hear this same bitter truth. As a nation, we long for virtuous people to welcome us, cherish us, soothe our pain, and protect us from evil ambition. Our failure to find these long-awaited ones is the root of all our sufferings. We long for thoughtful people who will put aside their pleasures for the sake of others. How many such heroes have there been in our recent history? How many people can you point to who comprehend the mystery of their own existence and embrace the responsibility of representing the Creator on earth?

We are desperately seeking such people of the heart; for they are also the people of truth, committed to transcendence. They inquire after the riddles of life, directing their questions to every part of existence and expecting answers from the infinite. They pursue truth as if it were the water of life. Wherever they find it, they savor its refreshment and attain immortality. They establish in themselves the universe of faith, wisdom, and love. They are heavenly in their appearance, and

---

[66] Said Nursi (d. 1960).

transcendent in their inwardness. They are like a tongue that expresses the true meaning of events and translates them into the language
of the conscience. They are the ones who reach new paradises within
themselves.

No one in our recent history has been able to fill this role. For we
act as if we are indifferent to the truth, ignorant of our own depths,
and unable to interpret the book of the universe. Many charlatans have
appeared to mock us, like imposters who find their way to the stage.
But they have not won our loyalty and will never be mistaken for the
expected ones.

We are ready to embrace the people of wisdom and thought. They
hold the gems of meaning fast in contemplation. They ascend to angelic heights, where they witness the mystery of their spiritual origin.
They can perceive the sun in an atom or the ocean in a drop. In them,
there is no quarrel between spirit and matter. As they study, they are
purified by wisdom and elevated by faith. Through their spiritual pleasure, Paradise is brought into the heart of humanity.

These awaited people side with the truth and stand with the community. They are sincere in all their actions: Their voices echo the
concerns of the society, and no ego dominates their feelings. They do
not boast of their achievements or celebrate their own victories. When
they succeed, they are filled with the noblest feelings. Neither personal concerns nor the interests of their coterie can sully their purposes.
Hatred and enmities cannot cloud their vision; love, forgiveness, and
tolerance are always secure in their gaze.

But those who want to bring "happiness" to humanity by the means
of violence and bloodshed; they are certainly the miserable ones, who
continue along the path that all divine scriptures reject.[67] I wish our
nation would discern the falsity of this deviation. Perhaps we would
then be done with these pests. Alas! Today, we are far from such discernment.

February 1980

---

[67] The author refers to the leaders and actors of the violent social and political movements in Turkey around the year of publication of this essay.

The Architects of Our Future

The intellectual laborers who will lay the foundations of the future are those fortunate ones who live the life of the soul. They are the champions of truth, submitting body to spirit. But they only appear indistinctly, faintly; whoever expects worldly pomp to announce their advent will be disappointed. Outwardly they are plain, but in their hearts burn countless bundles of incense giving off a variety of beautiful scents. It is difficult to speak of their beauty to those who have never known them, for: "He who does not taste does not know."[68] It would be easier to lift a mountain than to introduce the ignorant to this spiritual joy.

These architects of our future do not know fame or glory, nor do they wish for position or status. They are content with the light of infinity within them. In their soul, the universe is illuminated, but they do not appropriate this light for their own benefit. They are dedicated to service, saying: "Our task is to pave walkways; let others walk comfortably. Our duty is to struggle; let the trophy go to others." I wonder whether words can ever articulate the mystery of their essence.

Always modest and plain, they refuse any garrulous display and do not need special venues or high stages to proclaim their ideas. They communicate most effectively when deep feelings are reflected sincerely in their faces. Their essence is a lofty composite of matter and meaning; they do not reject their human nature but instead refine their body, as if it were lacework at the command of their spirit.

They endure suffering and do not know resentment. The flames of hatred and anger that threaten tolerance leave no trace on them. In the word of Yunus, they have no fists to punish the fighter, no tongue to answer the swearer, and no heart to be broken. Their soul is like a

---

[68] A Turkish and Arabic proverb.

puzzle in which thousands of concerns and thousands of joys fit perfectly together. Although remarkably altruistic, they are indifferent to their own well-being. Inspired by the generous lives of the Prophets, they are preoccupied with the pleasures and sorrows of others. They exist wholly for others, not for themselves.

They are determined and diligent; neither beauty nor prosperity can distract them from their purpose. In their sight, prestige is a deceptive and unbalanced scale, status is as ephemeral as writing on ice, and wealth is worth no more than a heap of straw in the wind. They set their heart on unfading beauties, and fleeting things cannot attract their gaze. Even the beauties of Paradise cannot distract them from their purpose. They treat fame and repute with disdain. Every battle in the name of honor is like a comedy to them, every struggle for glory like a quixotic quest. They do not need any prizes or accolades, because they are content with the heavenly honor: *"He has called you 'Muslims'— those who submit to God."*[69] To seek a glory beyond this would be an insult to our human essence.

They are the heroes of the heart: Their inwardness is radiant, their feelings are pure, their thoughts are sweet and well-ordered like a honeycomb, and their demeanor is like a paradise of peace. Anyone who encounters them finds happiness, and those who are far from them are far from peace. The architects of our future are free and unconfined; no mortal rope can bind their necks. For like pheasants, they already bear the most elegant mark: They have been bound to God.[70] In their captivity, they find freedom and say with the poet:

> *I have become a servant, become a servant, become a servant.*
> *I have bowed to You and doubled myself over.*
> *Slaves rejoice when they are freed;*
> *Whereas I rejoice when I become Your servant.*[71]

---

[69] Qur'an, 22:78.

[70] Pheasants have a natural rope-like color on their neck. The author uses this allegory to signify total submission to God.

[71] Rumi (d. 1273), the great Sufi master and poet of the Turko-Persian tradition of the Anatolian Seljuks.

Ambitions cannot pollute their intention, and lust can have no place in their world. Their nights are as pure as the morning; their days are pristine as Paradise.

For many years, our nation has waited heartsick for these architects to appear. We cannot know how much longer the wait will be. However, without losing hope, we will face the horizon and expect the sun to rise. We will continue to implore the Infinitely Merciful One; may He not prolong our time of waiting.

September 1980

The New Man

The cycles of history have brought us to the threshold of a new age, one that is open to the manifestations of God's providence. In the Muslim world, the recent centuries have been characterized by alienation, by the unconscious striving after intellectual fantasies, by opposition to traditional values, the denial of self identity, and confusion. But signs emerging all around us suggest that the twenty first century will be a time of faith, the age of our renaissance.

From out of the fickle crowds of our time, a truly new man will appear: a man, who thinks, reflects, and puts trust in both reason and inspiration. He will pursue perfection in all aspects of life, committing himself to comprehensive and holistic ideals. He will fly balanced on the wings of this world and the next in a successful marriage of heart and mind. Surely, the birth of this new man will not be easy, for pains and travails attend every birth. But when the time comes, a radiant new generation will suddenly be born among us. Like the rain that pours mercifully from dark and heavy clouds, or the waters that well up from the depths of the earth, or the blooms that burst forth as the snow blanket melts, these new men and women will surely come.

The new man will be full of integrity, determined to maintain his unique identity against all improper influences. Nothing will be able to limit his vision and movement, and no foreign ideologies will distract him from his spiritual path. His thought, his will, and his imagination will be completely free. He will be free in all things because he will serve only God, rejecting the slavish emulation of others and forging his own identity through his commitment to traditional virtues.

The new person will search, reflect, and believe. He will value spirituality and be filled with spiritual pleasures. In establishing his own identity, he will demonstrate his distinctiveness by subordinating the technological means of his time to the perennial values of his tradition. He will be inspired by the lofty personalities that constitute his glorious heritage, and configure his beliefs and thoughts accordingly. He will enthusiastically practice his values everywhere, never abandoning contemplation. Instead, he will passionately dedicate his life to the establishment of truth. Without concern for felicity and prosperity, he will readily give up everything he possesses for the sake of this cause. Like one who sows seeds in the bosom of the earth, he will pour out everything he has been given for the sake of his people and actively anticipate their future prosperity.

The new person will be part of the new generation and will utilize all possible means for reaching the minds and hearts of people, from publication to mass media. This generation of new men and women will represent their values everywhere and restore international dignity to their people. Although deeply spiritual, these new men and women will engage with all aspects of the modern world. This generation will demonstrate mastery in all human endeavors, from science to the arts, from technology to metaphysics. Their love of knowledge will be insatiable, their passion for wisdom will be renewed every day, and their spiritual depths will be beyond imagination. They will be like the enlightened people of the past, competing with the angels as they ascend toward God.

The new man will be filled with love for all creation. He will guard the human virtues, seek guidance from the moral principles that make us human, and find himself in them. He will be so universal that he will embrace the whole of existence with compassion. The new man chooses his way of life and seeks to shape society accordingly. He will protect what is good in his community and encourages others to do so. He will struggle vigilantly against evil until the day it is removed from society. He will encourage everyone toward faith and promote education. To him, service to God is beautiful, and he will practice it fully. He will support the social services that respect spiritual values and engage fully with public life. He will always advocate for the people and will bear the mark of responsibility among his community.

The new man will be filled with the creative spirit, despising formalism and clichés. He will find renewal in a return to his essential humanity. He will take responsibility for the course of time and walk ahead of his era, looking always toward the future. He will work with supernatural effort and yet rely absolutely on the strength of God. He will be so vigilant in his obedience to the laws of nature and to the will of God that the ignorant might mistake him for a naturalist or a fatalist. But he will always be a man of balance, observing the laws of causality and submitting to God, as his faith requires.

The new man will be a conqueror and a discoverer: Every day, he will carry his flag deeper into his soul and further toward the immensities of the universe, charging the gates of both the inner and outer worlds. His faith and wisdom will give him the confidence to approach the metaphysical reality beneath phenomena, and he will establish his headquarters in the realms beyond. Finally, when the grave calls him and he goes to receive his bounties, the heavens will not hesitate to welcome him.

March 1991

Devout Architects of Our Souls

Although people today denigrate the inner depths of the heart and belittle the importance of spiritual life, there is no doubt these are the true treasures of humanity. Regardless of what some skeptics may think, the life of inwardness is the only solution to our present social, political, and economic crises. This spiritual life can only be practiced by the devout ones, who are not concerned with their own felicity and who understand that their own prosperity is intimately tied to the prosperity of others.

Our salvation in the sight of God is contingent upon our own effort to save others: This is the true meaning of Islam. In order to secure our future in this world and in the Hereafter, we must become a refuge for other souls, strengthening their resolve and enlivening their hearts. We must be the ones who confront the challenges of our time, turning our backs on personal interest. Indeed, the moral character of actions will be measured against this ideal of responsibility.

The spirit of responsibility transcends our individual concerns and constitutes the most fundamental element of the universal order. Consequently, universal responsibility is the foundation for universal peace; it forms the unique essence of our salvation. This desire to help, support, and guide society lies at the very heart of public service. When we speak in the eloquent language of our shared responsibility, we inspire humanity with spirit and meaning.

There is no salvation for those who are indifferent to the universal order of existence, who spend their lives in the dark labyrinths of the ego. For not only do they perish, but they lead others to perish as well. Human progress occurs when we walk in harmony with the order of existence. Today, those who wish to participate in the building of the future should abandon egotism and realize their interdependence, for our individual ideals are only valuable when they become part of a shared conscience. Indeed, to live with others, and to live for others, our ego must first melt away. This is how we attain immortality: We constitute a community while yet remaining individuals; we become an ocean and yet remain distinct drops.

To fulfill the purpose of our creation, we must heed the commands of our hearts and not be distracted by our animal natures and trivial worries. To better know ourselves and our world, we must view all things through the eyes of the heart and judge generously, according to its criteria. If we cannot guard the purity of our souls or the vigor of our hearts, we will not inspire trust in the people around us. If we cannot remain as innocent as children, then no matter how rich our mental capacity or how vast our knowledge, we will not be of any help to others. This is why the majority of people obey politicians out of fear instead of trust, for they judge them to value power more than sincerity and to prioritize political authority over human feeling.

A person with a pure soul is recognized by the cleanliness of his thoughts and the honesty of his actions. In the Islamic tradition, the heart that remains pure is considered a house of God, a place where we discover Him hidden like a treasure. The more immaculate this house, the more one will encounter the divine truth there. It is in this sense that the heroes of spirituality have proclaimed, "I have seen the Truth!" These pure souls discover the gardens of Paradise in themselves: Their hearts contain the seed of the Tuba tree.[72] Capable of discerning the universe in a single atom, such souls approach the horizon of the Divine.

The Qur'an describes these people of the heart as heroes of truth who think, perceive, and act with conscience. They speak gently, demonstrate mercy, and behave with refinement. They lead others to an intimate knowledge of creation, expressing the true meaning and purpose of life. These devout ones strive to offer the elixir of infinity to every soul. They exist simultaneously in the depths of their own selves and in the furthest reaches of the external world, in their own hearts

---

[72] As mentioned earlier, Muslims believe the Tuba tree to be an eternal, glorious tree in Paradise.

and in the presence of their Lord. They hold fast to this apparent contradiction by denying their personal interests completely. Their sacrificial hearts are like those of the Prophets, and they promote the happiness of their neighbors without regard for their own physical needs. They work diligently to build their community, as if it were an ever-expanding pattern of embroidery, and they suffer alongside all humanity as they continue to work for peace.

They struggle against the evils that plague the world, particularly those faced by their own nation. They do not waste their efforts describing injustice, for this will only mislead pure minds. Instead, they actively design solutions. With the heroic resolve of the Prophets, they tackle the problems of their day out of a love of duty, a strong sense of responsibility, and a constant awareness of God. Impotent and poor before God, they learn to rely fully on His power and wealth. Enthusiastic and thankful toward Him, they feel the burden of their responsibility toward others. This responsibility is all-encompassing: Neither nature nor society, governance or security, the past or the future, the living or the dead, the young or the old, the learned or the ignorant is exempt from it. The people of the heart feel in their soul the hardship, even the agony, of such responsibility; their dedication is painful, and their obligation to others is always first in their minds. Here is the true spiritual ascension that brings us close to God and is valuable in His sight.

The suffering that accompanies this responsibility is a prayer that will never be rejected. For sincere consciences, it is a powerful impetus toward purity. The magnitude of this suffering inspires people of the spirit to work beyond their own ability; thus, they embody the potential of all past and future generations. Here we should remember the difference between those who live for themselves and those who live for others. Those who live for others are always sincere, loyal, and generous. They neglect themselves in order to better serve others. They are the true inheritors of the perennial truths, to whom we can entrust our souls. They do not desire to be followed, but their spiritual wealth is such an irrepressible invitation that, no matter where they are, people run to commit their souls to them.

The future will be the result of their devout work, a display of their responsibility and accomplishment. Our nation, our civilization, and our culture will be carried into the future on the shoulders of these faithful ones, for they are the trustees of lofty truths, the possessors of our rich heritage, and the true architects of our souls.

As heirs of history, they will guard the past as if it were a treasure, enrich our traditions through their own effort, and deliver our culture to the generations of the future. If devout ones do not fulfill this historic task, both the present and the future are a waste. If they surrender to indolence, if they neglect their responsibility, if they distract themselves with the beauties of Hereafter, they will have failed at their task and betrayed the trust of our history.

If our nation is to continue, we must assume the future to be ours. If we do not hold fast to this confidence, we dishonor our predecessors and disappoint our nation. It is high time that we support all our institutions of religion, science, art, morality, economy, and family; that we awaken them to the dignity of our history. As nation, we look for people of good will and determination who will take up this responsibility.

We do not need the aid of foreign ideologies or favors from other nations. We need physicians of spirit and thought, who can enliven in our people an awareness of their responsibility. We need those who will not simply promise us fleeting enjoyment but will illuminate the depths of our souls, those who can inspire us toward a spirituality that sees beyond the present. We are waiting for these devout individuals who so cherish their responsibility that they would even give up Paradise in order to fulfill it—the kind of people who will say: "If the sun is put in my right hand and the moon in my left, still I will not abandon my task."[73] This is the spiritual commitment of God's Prophets. Enraptured by the light of their horizon, they passionately say: "In my eyes I have neither love of Paradise nor fear of Hell; if I see the faith of my people secure, I will be ready to be burned in Hell-

---

[73] Prophet Muhammad, peace and blessings be upon him, is reported to have said this when Meccan polytheists offered him rewards, if he would cease conveying the message of the new faith.

fire."[74] Opening their hands, they plead: "O Lord, make my body so great that I alone fill up Hell and thus no place may be left for others."[75] This is a prayer that can shake the heavens.

Today, humanity desperately needs people of such spiritual depth: people who cry for the sins of others, who expect the forgiveness of humanity before their own forgiveness, who would stay in A'raf if it meant that others could enter Paradise,[76] who, even if they entered Paradise, would be too preoccupied with service to enjoy its bounties!

April 1995

---

[74] This is attributed to Said Nursi.

[75] This is attributed to Abu Bakr, the great Companion of the Prophet and the first caliph after him.

[76] Literally meaning "heights," A'raf refers to a place between Paradise and Hell, where a group of people will stay on the Day of Judgment. (See Qur'an, 7:46-49)

The Souls Devoted to God

For those who dedicate their lives to loving God, the attainment of His pleasure is their ultimate aim. These devoted ones do not expect anything, either material or spiritual, in return for their service: This is their most remarkable feature and their most important source of power. They do not take into account the values of this temporal life; profit, labor, and prosperity mean nothing to them.

Such souls are devoted to ideals far loftier than the values of the world. Since they are singly focused on God's good pleasure, it is difficult to divert them from their goal. They have undergone an ultimate transformation and have stripped away every ephemeral thing from their hearts. Thus, their character is unchanging. They have dedicated themselves entirely to the ideal of service; they care only to help others love God and be loved by Him. They bind their lives to the lives of others and shed all temporal expectations; they work for what is more precious than worldly reward. Such dedication establishes unity in them, not dispersion. As a result, they are far removed from the cheap antagonisms of society that try to divide "us" from "them." They have no problems with anyone, they take great pains to avoid conflict with their community, and they always think of how to help those around them. When they address society's problems, they speak as mentors, not warriors, inspiring others to live virtuously. They avoid political influence and run from any opportunity to rule over others.

In every aspect of life, these devoted souls apply their virtue and knowledge. They give their knowledge meaning by expressing it through action, according to the depth of their inner strength. In this way, they are tireless guides to whoever would emulate their human virtues. But they never think of personal gain, and they run from worldly praise as if they were fleeing scorpions and snakes. The wealth of their inwardness needs no advertisement or embellishment. Their behavior, which arises out of and reflects their spirit, is sweet enough to attract anyone with a refined palate. Therefore, they have no desire to boast, nor do they need eloquent words to inflate their value. They are not ambitious for renown, but they endeavor with all their strength toward a life of the heart and spirit. They seek God's pleasure in all their actions, exerting great effort toward this lofty goal. Like the Prophets before them, they care nothing for worldly favors.

Today, the foundations of our faith are under attack, and we should direct our every effort toward protecting them.[77] We must support people in their religious feelings and thoughts, for these alone will rescue them from aimlessness and inspire them to greatness. Faith must be revitalized in the hearts of our people. In a time when others intend to change the traditional structure of society, we must once again direct people toward the spiritual life. This is crucial, for if society is separated from its traditional moorings, conflict and division will proliferate. But spiritual reorientation will always bring about agreement and cooperation.

Those souls devoted to God's pleasure experience no emptiness in their mental life due to their singularity of purpose. They are always receptive to reason and science, for true faith requires such an attitude. Their worldly ambitions and corporeal desires melt away as each progresses toward God according to his capacity. Those desires are replaced by a distinct spiritual delight that originates in God's good pleasure. Therefore, though these devoted souls may commune with angels in their hearts, they can cooperate with anyone, fulfilling the legitimate requirements of life in the world. In this regard, they are both worldly and otherworldly. Their worldliness grounds them in the realm of natural laws, and they too must observe the limitations of the physical world. But their otherworldliness allows them to measure everything according to their heart's spiritual reality.

The spiritual life prohibits worldliness to a certain extent, but it does not completely abandon the world, and those devoted to God's

---

[77] This paragraph refers to the anti-religious regulations in Turkey that were enforced during the so-called "28 February Process," the uneasy years following the military ultimatum by memorandum on February 28, 1997.

pleasure should never be separated from the world. On the contrary, they stand at its very center, directing its course as God's representatives. But they do not adopt such a stance for the sake of the world itself. Rather, it is in order that we could relate everything to the world to come. In this, our bodies find their proper limit, and our spirit learns its true horizon. Nature is the appropriate domain for bodily life. But the horizon of spiritual life should be directed boundlessly toward infinite realities, for this is its nature. If we consistently engage with lofty thoughts, if we commit our lives to the One who has granted them, if we regard others as more important than ourselves, and if we always seek the summits of spirituality, then we will also learn the appropriate limit of our personal pleasures.

A life of such spiritual depth may sound difficult, but for those who give themselves to God, the task is easy. They have made service the purpose of their life, and they work tirelessly so that everybody can meet God. These souls live constantly at the threshold of the hearts of others and are always at the gate of the Divine. No duty is difficult for someone who, filled with awe and pure love, puts his faith in the Creator and speaks from his heart. Such a hero of the heart dedicates his attention to God, thinks only of Him, and takes every opportunity to become closer with Him. In response, God grants him special favors, reveals to others his privileged position, and rewards his fidelity with heavenly compliments. To mention a single example, God commands us to generously welcome the faithful no matter their social position, saying: *"Do not drive away those who call upon their Lord morning and evening, seeking nothing but His Face."*[78]

If your devotion is sincere and genuine, God will always grant you special favors. Your work will receive divine acknowledgement, and you will become a subject of heavenly conversations, according to the degree of your commitment to God. But first, you must make God's pleasure the ultimate purpose of your life. Then, the sincerity of your thoughts, words, and actions will secure for you a luminous paradise in world to come. Indeed, those who fill their sails with the winds of

---

[78] Qur'an, 6:52.

their good fortune will cruise smoothly toward God, carried along by breezes of divine favors. The Qur'an's depiction of such fortunate ones is worthy of contemplation:

> Such men are not distracted, either by commerce or profit, from remembering God, keeping up the prayer, and paying the pre-scribed alms, for they fear a day when hearts and eyes will turn over. God will reward such people according to the best of their actions, and He will give them more of His bounty: God provides limitlessly for anyone He will.[79]

In submission to God, these devoted souls rid themselves of the burdens of worry and grief, thus attaining freedom. Nothing is hidden from them. Compared to their attainments in their spiritual realm, the fleeting blessings and pleasures of this world are no more than empty bowls left on a dirty table. What are the transient contents of this physical world compared to the eternal beauties reflected in the world of their heart? Does nature not turn green in the spring and grow pale in the summer? But souls oriented toward eternity reject everything that does not promise everlasting togetherness with God. Their hearts move toward the gardens of the infinite, and neither this world nor its many distractions can cause them to stumble.

October 2000

---

[79] Qur'an, 24:37-38.

CHAPTER SIX

ISLAM

The Nature of Islamic Religion

There are two sides to the love of truth: One is science, conceived in the broadest sense, and the other is religion.[80] Consciousness and the universe are related through our discovery of reality on the one hand and our attitude toward it on the other. The former is the subject of science, which also includes the study of religious knowledge, while the latter is shaped by religion itself. A science that is not founded on the analysis of existence and guided by the love of truth suffers from its lack of vision, and its findings cannot escape contradiction. Science pursued for some personal interest will certainly come to an impasse. Likewise, knowledge that is biased toward a particular philosophy or doctrine will inevitably cause confusion. Religion, particularly Islam, offers distinct sources of knowledge and is equally an expression of the love of truth. With regard to matters beyond the boundaries of natural science, religion is a sure guide: clear in its style and profound in its method.

Unfortunately, science is too often subordinated to particular philosophies or doctrines, thus narrowing its focus. In this way, science becomes an obstacle to truth. Even religion, our heavenly reality, can become a source of hatred in the hands of fanatics. What a paradox that a thing may become its opposite! Imagine a school of science: In its natural essence, it is as sacred as a temple, but it capitulates to a particular worldview. In the hands of such a school, science becomes a site of bigotry and prevents freedom. Science thus condemns itself, becoming more inauspicious than even the most cursed ignorance. And imagine a religion that has been made a vehicle for certain narrow interests; this temple then becomes little more than a political chamber,

---

80 The author uses *ilim* (originally *ilm* in Arabic) to refer to "science." Also meaning "knowledge," *ilim* traditionally denotes all systematic studies, namely all disciplines that we now assign to natural and social sciences and also humanities.

and worship deteriorates into formalism. The transcendence of both religion and the religious life is diminished.

If we proclaim "science," but use our schools solely to promote ambition and ideology, then these schools are no longer sacred places. They are merely arenas in which we sharpen our desires, ambitions, and hatred. If we proclaim "piety" but slander those with whom we do not agree, calling them infidels and hypocrites, then our places of worship actually alienate people from God and darken their hearts. This is not the purpose of revelation! The enmity against religion that exists today is a form of bigotry that would please Satan. But fists raised in religion's defense are just as bad; when we attack the opinions of others, we display an ignorance that would grieve the angels.

If a person does not know true faith or heed conscience when it speaks, if he is bereft of divine love, if he does not treasure what is precious to God, then that person is not truly religious, regardless of appearances. To mistake appearance for true religion is to insult the universal essence of religion itself. Our desires and ambitions will undermine both science and religion if we mistake them for empirical findings or present them as if they are piety. This is our basic human weakness: We desire to appear greater than we are, and we expect to receive more than we deserve. If religion or science is lauded by society, we too easily seek to hide our weaknesses behind their esteem. In other words, we use religion and science to fill the gaps in our own character. Against this human weakness, our most powerful armor is the love of truth. Indeed, if there is an elixir that could remove this rust from our minds and hearts, it is the love of truth. When our souls are enraptured with this love, our human weaknesses melt away.

The love of truth leads us to God and establishes our connection with creation. This love was first practiced by the Prophets, and it was through their guidance that humanity embraced it. Since the beginning, every Prophet of God has led humanity like a commander of love. Their movements form embroidered patterns on love's canvas. Their individual existences dissolve into the pool of divine love: this is the true value of their mission. The life of Jesus was a poem that proclaimed the love of humanity in every form. Prophet Muhammad, the Pride of Humanity, peace and blessings be upon him, demonstrated the truth of Fuzuli's poem: "My word is the flag-bearer of the army of lovers."[81] His life gave voice to this divine love, and when his love could be contained no longer, he walked to the Hereafter with his eyes fixed upon its eternal manifestations. The Qur'an is a message of love, if it is read with faith and attention. It is the convergence of longing and reunion. The passion for truth, the love of knowledge, the work of research and serious inquiry, the discipline of contemplation: these are the subjects of its every chapter. The Qur'an beckons to believers like a diamond deposit, in which curious explorers discover new treasures with every visit. Rapt in the indescribable pleasures of thought, everyone who searches the Qur'an carefully unearths new wonders.

With its rich content, the Qur'an is uniquely capable of relieving our sufferings and curing our centuries-old wounds. But sadly, its representatives today are poor in spirit. Their passion is not for the truth, their learning is superficial, and their judgments are twisted. They do not practice self-interrogation, but prefer to criticize others. They privilege self-interest, promote ambition over reason, and care more about their appearance than their inner depths. Such a misrepresentation of the Qur'an's message, compounded by a general lack of interest in religion today, obscures its perfect purity and instills doubt in hesitant souls. With their eyes blinded by material interests, these false faithful cannot comprehend, let alone reflect, the magnificent universe of the Qur'an, imbued with spirit and meaning. Even if they possess all the trappings of transcendence, they will not comprehend its profound message.

The Qur'an is a profound teaching of balance. It offers its adherents a path leading toward universal harmony, in which the relationships among the individual, the family, the society, and the created world achieve equilibrium. But the narrowness of our own logic has limited the vast, localized the universal, and reduced the transcendent to the ordinary. Thus, we have allowed the Qur'an's glory to be eclipsed again and again. The great figures of Islamic history, such as Said ibn

---

[81] Fuzuli (d. 1556), a great Turkic-Ottoman poet.

Jubayr, Abu Hanifa, Ahmad ibn Hanbal, and Sarakhsi, left behind a legacy that preserves the true spirit of the Qur'an.[82] They would never concede to injustice or oppression, much less promote it. Their judgments were always rooted in their conscience, which was always open to God. They chose the suffering of prison over the pleasures of the palace. They chose freedom in thought and conscience, a freedom that finds its true depth in service to God.

Those who live purposefully will die with a purpose. When they die, they will be laid to rest in our memory, our shared conscience, where they will remain forever. But unlike such lofty souls, the slaves to personal interest do not care about anything serious and remain blinded by their own desires. They live in misery, the legacy they leave is a curse, and the only end they meet will be disaster upon disaster. However, a faithful disciple of the Qur'an, a person of ideals, leads the charge into the infinite. With his life of love, enthusiasm, excitement, and passion, he transcends that which others call reality; he is so courageous that dissolute souls assume him to be mad.

A lofty ideal is like a catapult: It can launch us beyond the obstacles of desires and ambition and into the spiritual realm. Those who fix their eyes on their ideal will be hurled into orbit like a rocket; they will assume their exalted place in the sight of God. Islam is an abundant spring that sustains this ideal person, and the Prophet is his compassionate attendant. He is the most faithful representative of Islam and its timeless interpreter, for he brings us the interpretations that suit this revelation's heavenly origin. In this regard, he is like a guide, indicating to his followers what is most perfect and most human. He is a reformer, a legislator, and a revolutionary; and the doctrine he established will extend far into the future. Whoever does not appreciate the wisdom of the Qur'an or accept the Prophet as its most skillful exegete cannot attain the truth of Islam. In the life of such unfortunate ones, religion is nothing but mythologies and antiquated thinking; it becomes a monstrosity riddled with dross and at odds with its time.

---

[82] These historical and respected Muslim scholars are well known with their plain lifestyle, dedication to social justice, and advocacy for human rights. They were oppressed and imprisoned by the governments of their respective times.

The Qur'an is a spring so deep and immense, so pure and abundant, that it is beyond the comprehension of all who approach it. It is thus a source of spiritual satisfaction for all. As our understanding flourishes, the Qur'an becomes to us like a rainbow, always just beyond our grasp. As for the true religious life, it is a transcendent rendering that originates in the Qur'an and shapes us. Those who genuinely follow this religion will experience its inimitable beauty: simple as our everyday life, yet more perfect than we can imagine.

November 1997

Resting in the Shade of Islam

To rest in the shade of Islam is to be honored with divine blessings. Those who do not have the good fortune of the Qur'an's guidance cannot enjoy the charms of this life. But those who know the Qur'an in its uniqueness live as if they were in the courtyards of Paradise, smiling at all their surroundings. They thank God for the shelter of Islam and reflect on the world around them in gratitude. All that they see and hear reminds them of the Qur'an and causes them to murmur its verses. They feel the deep pleasures of contemplation and are enraptured by the progression of their own thoughts toward God.

The Qur'an teaches us to perceive and interpret the truth in phenomena. Those who live in the shade of Islam take pleasure in what they understand, and what they do not understand, they submit to God. Therefore, they never face consistent distress, chaos, or depression. In joyous times, they give thanks and praise to God, and so their joy becomes even more meaningful. As for adversity and tribulation, events that appear bitter and sour are softened by the wisdom: "This too will pass!" In the shade of Islam, the devout are weaving colorful lattice-works of gratitude, even in the darkest of times. Whoever visits them and experiences their calm presence will know the peace and joy of the people of Paradise.

If our lives thoroughly represent the depths, hues, and patterns of Islam and if we are engaged with the Qur'an, we will be elevated to distinction and becoming truly otherworldly. We will understand the purpose of existence, the wisdom present in creation, the mystery and meaning of human life, the privilege of our responsibility to nature, and the value of what is to come. We will feel ascend the luminous helix grounded in our heart to the horizon of reality, where we under-

stand the nature of the Eternal One. We will marvel at our good fortune and say to ourselves: "This must be life!"

Many people are terrified by the appalling events of our time, but
in the shade of Islam, we comprehend operation of the universe as its
obedience to God. Thus, this vast universe becomes like a home to
us: We feel familiarity toward every object, share love with every creature, and thank God for granting us such happiness. In the shade of the
Qur'an, creation is more diverse, more abundant, and more meaningful than its appearance. It is as if the world is unveiled, as if we are
observing a realm beyond this three-dimensional space. Even if this
revelation is not shared by everyone, we all discover the world to be
much wider than it first appears, according to the richness of faith in
our hearts. Unlike those who slouch from depression to depression like
prisoners, we take shelter in the promise of a happy future like the
honored guests of a vast palace.

According to Islamic thought, this world, so spacious and enjoy-
able, is only one dimension of creation. The magnificence of the physical realm is but a curtain veiling the metaphysical beyond; the true
exhibitions of beauty lie in the realms beyond appearance. In Islamic
thought, everything originates in the metaphysical realm, appears in
this natural world, and persists in the Hereafter. This natural world is
only a station on the way; its blessings are appetizers of the coming
feast. Our journey will take us far beyond this world: We will glimpse
our eternal future from the intermediate realm of the grave, we will
enter the great field of the Last Judgment with trembling, and we will
proceed to either the lofty garden of eternal beauties or to a horrible
abyss. Paradise, described for its surprises by the Prophet as a place "no
eyes have seen, no ears have heard, no minds have imagined," is the
last stop of our long journey.

From this eternal perspective, a Muslim sees everything differently, evaluates everything differently, and displays this difference in all
his manners. He knows that he is God's vicegerent on earth and that
everything is at his disposal. This truth echoes deep in his conscience:

"Your Lord told the angels: I am setting on the earth a vicegerent."[83] He bows in utmost gratitude to God in the face of this special task: *"He has put all that is in the heavens and the earth at your service."*[84] This honor arises from the timeless depths, and he welcomes it with joy, as if he were the first ever to receive it. He regards all that has been granted to him thus far as a glimpse of what will be his in the future. So he runs breathlessly along the path of the Prophets. On this way, he never fails to put his trust in God, and he carefully obeys the order established by the Creator. Even though he works diligently, he knows that the result of his effort comes from God. His life is well-balanced, for he trusts in God while honoring the laws of nature. He remains conscious of God's protection and breathes easily with peace, security, and satisfaction. How pleasant is this comfort of the heart! How joyous is life at such a spiritual horizon!

To rest in the shade of Islam is to turn your heart toward God. It is fair to say that this life of rest has the power to remove corruption from the earth and establish peace among nations. Islam is the lost peace we have been longing for, and in it we discover the harmony between human and natural life that society was created to reflect. If humanity today is unable to recognize Islam's promises, this is as much the fault of our own unfaithfulness to its messages as it is the fault of the hostility and prejudices of our opponents. In saying, *"We reveal the Qur'an as healing and mercy,"*[85] God Almighty reminds us that this Book is a remedy for all of our afflictions, and He calls upon us to turn to it for healing. With His word, *"This Qur'an does indeed show the straightest way,"*[86] God offers us a mysterious key that will open any gate.

Nonetheless, many of us succumb to neglect or ignorance and fail to utilize this priceless key. In daily life, when our simple devices break, we do not hesitate to call an expert or return them to their manufacturer for repair. But we often fail to follow this same procedure in regard

---

[83] Qur'an, 2:30.
[84] Qur'an, 45:13.
[85] Qur'an, 17:82.
[86] Qur'an, 17:9.

to our spiritual life: We do not appeal to our Maker for instruction and advice. Clearly, the One who has made us must know how to repair us. As complex and valuable creatures, we should come to the All-Knowing Creator with both our inward and outward problems. He will refer us to the Qur'an for resolution and guidance: *"He knows the contents of every heart. How could He who created not know? He is the All-Knowing, All-Aware."*[87]

History will record humanity's current indifference toward Islam as our fault. Future generations will remember us and say, "If only they had been more discerning." But on that day, this regret will be of no use. It is vital that we discern the true promises of Islam and fulfill our historic mission. I wonder whether the generations of today, who share in this destiny, will be able to achieve it. I hope they can. Their return to Islam, to the spirit and meaning voiced by the Qur'an, will be their rebirth. Indeed, the Qur'an is a unique source of original ideas, ageless disciplines, and imperishable teachings concerning existence, life, and human virtues. We strongly believe that the Book of Islam will create new possibilities for today's societies, offer them alternative ways of thinking, and relieve their sufferings. But this is possible only if we truly re-imagine our place within existence and live according to our divine calling. After the long sleep of the past centuries, such a revival among Muslims would offer much to the rest of the world.

In the past, Muslim revivals have occurred because communities began to scrutinize both themselves and the universal laws of life; they reconciled the mysteries of nature with religious thought and discerned no contradiction between God's moral commandments and the rules of nature. Likewise, the dissolution of Muslim communities in history corresponds to their failure to sustain this reconciling synthesis. Our failure today to truly understand the relationship among humanity, the universe, and God has brought great affliction upon us. We face confusion and drift from one depression to another. Our deliverance from this evil situation will only come if we can rejuvenate Islamic thought in the light of contemporary knowledge and reenact the

---

[87] Qur'an, 67:13-14.

harmony between the laws of divine creation that govern the universe and the laws of religion that regulate our relationship to God. In our recent past, this potential for harmony has been overlooked, if not completely ignored. This led to the loss of stability in life and successive social troubles. Simply put, we distorted our harmonious relationship with existence and God revoked his blessings. This is an unchanging law of God, a divine habit: *"God never changes a favor He conferred on a people unless they change what is within themselves."*[88] The safest way to protect ourselves is thus to maintain a right relationship with both God and creation. So far, this important task has only been accomplished by the generations who have held fast to the Qur'an.

November 2000

---

[88] Qur'an, 8:53.

Characteristics of Islam

I slam is rooted in eternity, beyond time and space. It addresses the human heart, whose spiritual breadth encompasses the heavens and the earth, and its end is happiness in this world and the next. Islam is the straight path that extends throughout eternity. It is a system of thought sent from heaven to triumph in all hearts, beginning with the Prophet, the noblest of humanity, and thus to realize humanity's desire for eternal life.

Since Islam was first established on earth, it has directed all its energy toward this conquest of hearts. It places its signature in the conscience of humanity and marches into all aspects of our shared life. Islam's impact in our lives correlates to the depth at which it takes hold in our hearts. The more deep-rooted it is in our souls, the more abundant its influence will be in our life and environment. A society's orientation toward Islam is directly proportional to the commitment of individual believers to Islam as their inner reality. This spiritual reality will determine the direction of the moral, economic, political, and cultural life of society and reveal itself in every aspect of social life.

The fundamental message of Islam is: "There is no deity but God and Muhammad is His Messenger." These two short sentences proclaim both the absolute divine unity and the way to attain it. All matters of faith are expressed in this statement. The great tree of faith originates in this kernel of truth and spreads out toward the edges of our awareness, bearing the fruit of wisdom. In the end, an inner movement of perception transforms all of our knowledge into passionate love. This love encircles our existence and reshapes our conscience. This new spiritual existence manifests itself in the lover's every action: It is reflected in his worship and service, his social relations and work, and his cultural and artistic activities. In this way, the people of faith and wisdom always display the truth of their inner lives. They cannot help but express the love and spiritual delight inside them.

We may not always maintain the same degree of spiritual awareness, but our deeply-rooted beliefs will continue to direct our behaviors, whether we are aware of them or not. This inner dynamic naturally determines our lifestyle. In other words, the way we think about our place in existence, the purpose of our creation, and the responsibility that attends it will affect our entire consciousness. In time, these considerations will become second nature. In fact, it is this second nature that constitutes the framework of our true life. Having attained this level of spiritual discipline, we can be certain that our thoughts and actions will always be in the service of God. And, committed to this service, we will see every aspect of our lives flowing together like rivers cascading harmoniously to the sea.

Faith is the dynamo of people of spirit, and worship preserves and supports this faith. Morality and virtue are the clear marks of faith, but so too are culture and art. Islamic art embodies the quest for beauty in abstraction and emphasizes the transcendent divine unity against anthropomorphism and vulgar materialism. Its abstract character always accommodates new interpretations, thus we are able to discern the ocean in a single drop and speak volumes with a single word. As for Islamic culture, it addresses the entire scope of our human reality. We find in it everything that belongs to us, from the past to the present. We must continue to develop this cultural heritage and entrust it to future generations; our task today is to protect our traditions and strive to maintain our historical identity. We must remain faithful to our own beliefs by constantly enriching them with new considerations. We should depend on our Islamic heritage as much as possible and let it guide us in our own course. We must contemplate creation from within our own culture, always putting forward new ideas in the spirit of our great tradition.

Islam is completely open to the values of other traditions and cultures, so long as they are compatible with its own. Islam seeks, finds, and appropriates whatever is beneficial, regardless of its origin. In the ancient world, Islam adopted and utilized the scientific and technical developments of its time, preserving them for the future. It must do so again. Humanity is God's representative on earth, and so Muslims must study out of a deep love for truth and passion for knowledge and acquire expertise in every human endeavor. In religious studies, however, a subject that depends on the teachings of the Qur'an and the Prophet, Muslims should be committed to their own texts. But they should be ready and willing to participate in the natural and social sciences, for these are the heritage of all humanity and are not exclusive to a certain religious or cultural tradition. As we enjoy our own religious and cultural identity, we should always be ready to participate in, contribute to, and benefit from these common studies.

The history of Islamic civilization clearly shows that such a receptive attitude can prevent needless conflicts between religion and science. The Islamic experience is quite different from the Western experience in this regard. In the past centuries, the method and philosophy of scientific knowledge in Europe was at odds with religion, leading to a separation of mind and heart. This negative development seems to be a major cause of centuries-old crises in the social and cultural systems of the West. The scientific and philosophical front emerged as a reaction to church dogma that sought to stand in for religion itself. But in time, this reaction gave way to an ethos that opposed all religious traditions. In this way, a scientific and philosophical culture of atheism has become a threat to faith and piety all around the world. Despite its innocence, Islam has not been exempt from this antagonism. Islamic faith and piety have unjustly faced the attacks of the anti-religious movements motivated by the struggle between primarily Christian institutions and modern Western scientific circles, although Islamic civilization itself witnessed no such conflict.

Islam has always presented humanity with a unique way of life. When it first appeared, Islam was unprecedented, and as history progressed, it would prove to be matchless. It introduced principles that reordered human life, offered new interpretations of this world and the next, changed the relationship among God, humanity, and the universe, and put an end to contradictions in the concept of divinity. Islam brought value to both life and death. It answered the questions of humanity and left no intellectual, spiritual, logical, or emotional holes in the hearts and minds of its audience. Islam expanded and flourished as it was lived and practiced. It proved to be a dynamic system that did not delay in posing solutions to the problems of humanity. It penetrated every corner of life; it was at once individual, familial, social, economic, political, and cultural.

In its earliest formation, Islam was not "idealist," as this term is understood in Western philosophy. The sun of idealism rises over the unknown steppes of the Mount Qaf.[89] The rays of this sun do not reach the world of reality; they are refracted by dreams and lost in their own interpretation. On the contrary, Islam promised a *sui generis* system applicable to all areas of life. Those who heeded its call found in it a system that had developed in the same womb as their innermost human nature. From its establishment in individual conscience to its moral manifestations in public life, Islam left nothing untouched and left none of its followers helpless or weak.

Islam was first and foremost spiritual, and it began its life in the conscience of individuals. Once established there, it began to spill over to its surroundings, bringing with it a message of eternal existence and transforming all that it touched. Every message of Islam was a song of universal peace, a composition of social harmony, a hymn to tolerance and dialogue. Rudeness and hatred were found only in its enemies, or in those adherents ignorant of its truth. Despite its luminous nature, the glory of Islam has been periodically eclipsed by these shadows. If its enemies had ceased their hostility and its friends remained faithful to it, Islam would no doubt have removed the darkness of hatred and oppression from the earth and ushered in the trust and security of Paradise. War, murder, terror, and anarchy would have been erased from the earth and replaced with love, respect, harmony, and peace.

When Islam truly resides in the heart, there is only room in it for the love and tolerance of the Creator. Indeed, hatred and enmity cannot exist together with true faith and connection with God. If the heart

---

[89]   The Mount Qaf is a mythical mountain in Muslim tradition. Possibly adopted from the ancient Persian and Jewish mythologies, it was imagined to surround the world.

renews and strengthens this faith through various forms of worship, then it will be closed to animosity. Every Islamic act evokes in us the feeling that all of our acts should be Islamic; we are thus inspired to live faithfully. This spiritual growth is reflected in our behaviors and constitutes the fabric of our morality. It is the essential origin of our culture, and it secures our identity. Our spiritual perfection, based on faith and trust in God, influences our surroundings in the form of sincerity, love, and concern. Due to the power of this spiritual attraction, Muslims transcend their individuality and become a community. Just as artworks begin deep inside us before they appear in the external world, so do our moral behaviors, our society, and our culture. In other words, the elements of our internal life are the basic determinations of our external one.

Unlike other religious and philosophical systems, Islam introduces humanity to a system of life that has a universal dimension but is nevertheless particular to itself. For Islam requires its followers to practice and implement its teachings. Muslims conscious of this responsibility will strive to be faithful to Islamic values in all their individual and social relations. If an ideal is not embodied in action and movement, it remains as unreal as a dream. Likewise, the reality of faith inside us will persist to the degree that it is introduced into our daily practice and flourishes there. If our faith is exhibited in our actions, in the deep reverence of our worship and prayer, and in the truthfulness and integrity of our social relations, then our faith can be considered genuine. Such faith is not only an endless source of energy and strength for us; it is our inheritance as God's vicegerents on earth. It grounds our interventions into the natural world and gives us the spirit of creation.

Faith instills in the soul a deep appreciation for aesthetic value. In this spirit, a believer's art reflects the true nature of reality as perceived through the prism of eternity. The artist engraves a sense of eternity into his or her work in such a way that, whenever we contemplate it, we are presented with a miniature of the whole of existence. In art, we have the pleasure of observing the infinite from within the finite. Art is not rebellion according to Islam, nor is it an exhibition of talent.

Rather, it is a synthesis of the spirit and meaning of phenomena brought about by the language of the heart. Art expresses the truth that should always be before us, with a flexibility that enables us, through our contemplation, to perceive that truth in a new dimension. Art refers to the transcendent reality, the Unconceivable One, and thus demonstrates unity in plurality and plurality in unity.

In short, Islam is the recitation and interpretation of the book of the universe. It is the map of this universal reality, sketched on the past, present, and future. It is the mysterious key that unlocks creation's truth. Islam is a whole composed of all these, a whole irreducible to its many parts. It would be wrong to take Islam to pieces and then look for its meaning among them; this would betray its essential unity. Those who attempt to explain Islam with reference to the commentary of a couple of Qur'anic verses or Prophetic sayings will always be mistaken and will miss the magnificent corpus that is Islam as a whole. Their consciences will constantly be shaken by this great void in their souls.

Islam is faith, worship, morality, thought, knowledge, and art. It is a complete system of human virtue—a thorough, wonderful, heavenly feast presented to its attendees. It involves the whole of life, and it interprets life as a whole. It evaluates the reality of life and never cries out in despair. Islamic instruction is bound to practicality, and its judgments are not rooted in a world of dreams. Islam is dynamic and extends to all parts of life, from matters of creed to those of culture and art. This is the essential sign of Islam's own life and universality.

April 1999

A Partial Description of
Our System of Thought

Reason, experience, emotion, and revelation: all forms of human knowledge are integral to our system of thought, for they are all different facets of a single unity. This rich episte-mological foundation gives Islamic thought its incomparably vast reach. Islam's message to humanity is comprehensive: It is rooted in divine revelation, remains within the framework of human reason, respects human feelings, and is enriched by inspiration.[90] Islam's judgments concerning the relationships among humanity, the universe, and God are based in sound logic. No other systems of thought can maintain this same balance among reason, heart, and spirit.

Islam speaks to both our inner life and our relationships with the external world; thus, it is perfectly compatible with human nature. It is peerless in meeting the needs of humanity. And this is not surpris-ing, since Islam's primary source is divine revelation, and this revela-tion's first interpreter is the Prophet, peace and blessings be upon him. As the Qur'an is a miracle, so too is Islam, for it is constituted by the Qur'an's teachings. As the Qur'an is matchless, so too is Islam.

Once we enter the luminous world of the Qur'an, we begin to perceive the phenomena of this world differently. Our physical and spiri-tual senses deepen: Human reason sees everything as it is, our hearts grow and flourish under its nurturing guidance, and our spirit ascend the heavens of its own perfection, relating everything to itself. The prom-ises of the Qur'an have come true, are coming true, and will continue to come true for as long as believers cultivate its teachings in their

---

[90] In mainstream Islamic terminology, "revelation" (*wahy*) denotes God's special and clear communication with His Messengers, whereas "inspiration" (*ilham*) denotes an inferior and implicit communication to guide any people.

consciences and perceive them in the light of their original revelation. In fact, those with such perception have always found love and excitement in the Qur'an. Those who hear with the ears of their heart are thrilled by its call for spiritual revival.

The Qur'an introduced into the world a different concept of struggle. It speaks of our struggle to know ourselves, our struggle to engage with all of creation, our struggle to resist the snares of corporeality, and our struggle to master our inner world. We struggle to guard our hearts against animosity, hatred, lust, greed, and jealousy, and we struggle to dedicate ourselves to a lofty ideal. We struggle to transcend all fears and all expectations, to win the Hereafter by accepting this world, and to improve this world by acknowledging the Hereafter.[91]

This message of struggle was established by the Qur'anic revelation. Later, the message flourished "like a good tree whose roots are firm and whose branches touch the sky," transforming the Islamic world into a garden of Paradise.[92] In the years of this revelation, Qur'anic verses were cascading like waterfalls. They were the first fruits of the divine realm, gathered with excitement by eager hearts and souls. For those fortunate ones, every day was like a new heavenly banquet. In the presence of such an outpouring, humanity experienced multiple revivals, one after the other, and everyone who heard the divine word became like a Khidr, giving life to all they encountered.[93] God was calling on them to renew themselves in mind and heart, in feeling and in thought: *"O you who believe! Respond to God and His Messenger when you are called to that which gives you life."*[94] And they readily answered this divine call, saying: *"Our Lord! We have heard a Messenger calling us to faith: 'Believe in your Lord.' And we have believed. Our*

---

[91] Throughout this paragraph, "struggle" is originally *cihad*, the Turkish spelling of *jihad*, a word that is often mistakenly interpreted. The author suggests here how to understand that concept properly.

[92] For the quotation, see Qur'an, 14:24.

[93] As mentioned earlier, Khidr, the "Green One," is a spiritual personality in Islamic tradition. He is known for the "revival" effect of his presence, as implied in the Qur'an, 18:63-65.

[94] Qur'an, 8:24.

Lord! Forgive us our sins, wipe out our bad deeds, and let us join the righteous when we die."[95]

Their constant vitality can be attributed to the atmosphere in which they lived. They were immersed in the Qur'an, listening to it without prejudice and believing in it with their whole hearts. In response to this supreme book, they loved God whole-heartedly and endeavored to help others love Him. They guarded their thoughts and feelings against desire. Their entire character represented the truth of Islam, and thus they always found welcome with new audiences. In this luminous time, Islam and the Qur'an were understood by all. Anyone could easily comprehend the Qur'an, interpret it correctly, and see in it the greatness of God. There was no preoccupation with theoretical knowledge; on the contrary, people quickly put their new knowledge into practice. They cared more for embodiment than for the accumulation of information. In other words, their knowledge was transforming them into agents of divine action. They fully understood the purpose of their creation and found in their dedication to God the great pleasures they had vainly sought in material things. Freed from the narrow straits of corporeality, they could now set sail each day to new horizons in the vast ocean of the heart.

After this early period, sound interpretations of the Qur'an continued to flourish in Islamic history. Shaped by the teachings of the Qur'an and the dedication of believers, past societies have often borne witness to Islam's ideal system of life. Since humanity has achieved this ideal many times in the past, there is no reason that it cannot be realized again in the future. Time may change, but this ideal spirituality will always be attainable. In this regard, we can repeat the achievements of the past; Muslims need only to maintain their spirit of struggle, self-discipline, and awareness. They must live according to the heart, be alert against the weakness of their human nature, and protect their inner world from negativity.

In fact, one of the most important aspects of Islamic thought is its affirmation of temporal life, which other philosophies too often treat

---

[95] Qur'an, 3:193.

with scorn. Islam prefers to relate every aspect of this world to God, envisioning this world as an enviable courtyard of the Hereafter. In this sense, the world can be viewed as a field ready for cultivation or a harbor at the boundary of the world to come. Islam accepts the human individual as a whole and addresses all our physical, mental, and spiritual faculties. It is responsive to our wishes, provides for our natural needs, and delimits a context in which we can flourish.

There are essentially only two sources of knowledge and wisdom in Islam: the Qur'an and the Prophetic tradition. This makes it unique among other thought traditions. And since its beginning, Islam has kept its distance from the religious and philosophical heritage of antiquity in an effort to preserve its unique identity. Although Islam respects the authentic aspects of previous revelations—as Islamic jurisprudence demonstrates with its notion of *"shar'u man qablana"* or "the religious laws of those before us,"—it has always been committed to its own sources, the sources of fresh revelation. Islam is nurtured and nourished by the Qur'an and the Prophetic tradition; it does not need the heritage of ancient religious and philosophical thought, nor does it benefit from the fantasies of modern times. It does not appeal to the dreams of idealists, the arguments of rationalists, the method of positivists, or any other modern philosophies. Islam has never found them to be reliable sources of knowledge.

Islam offers methods, manners, and solutions that are without precedent in historical revelation or human thought. In all its aspects, Islam is an example of perfection. It considers the entirety of human existence: our physical, mental, and spiritual dimensions. It restores to the human being the richness of moral responsibility. Unlike many philosophical schools, Islam does not emphasize the mind at the expense of feeling, conscience, or humanity's other spiritual capacities. It does not limit man to any of the particularities of his existence. Instead, Islam looks at the human being with the eyes of the Creator. It embraces a unity that defies fragmentation and division, and trains humanity for happiness in this world and the next.

July 2000

The Last Messenger of the Unseen

The final word about God, the universe, and humanity was spoken by Prophet Muhammad, peace and blessings be upon him. He voiced the call to Truth, and he became the origin and final cause of all things through his unique service to God and humanity.[96] He is the last Messenger of the unseen, proclaiming its greatest secrets. He is the interpreter who never misleads, the one who teaches the true relationship between humanity and God, who clarifies our responsibilities. He is at once the first man and the last Messenger, the closest to God and our most reliable guide to divine closeness.

The angels awaited his advent, many Messengers brought the good news of his arrival, and even now, the eminent friends of God depend upon him. He lit the torch of Prophethood, and his life was made luminous by its truth. In this sense, his reflection of the divine glory gave the world its first light, and his appearance in the physical world was this light's final outpouring. As the universal Messenger, he is uniquely perfect: the index of internal and external realities, the essence and extract of the creation, the brightest fruit of the tree of existence, and the master of all humanity in the name of the Supreme Creator.

His essence is beyond description. He is matchless in his spiritual depths, and through his message, the Truth is manifest. His fame reaches back to the time before Adam; his light was legendary even before his existence. His coming was a divine bestowal, his existence was the pure pearl in the nacre of creation, and his message was addressed to all humanity. In him resides the abstract knowledge of all science, and

---

96 In Sufi metaphysics, the so-called "Muhammadan truth" (namely, the divine idea of the perfect human) is the essential norm of divine creation and hence the primordial origin of universal existence. Likewise, the person or mission of the Prophet, peace and blessings be upon him, is the special telos of creation.

his wisdom is a crystal clear spring around which the brightest faces gather. His spirit is the tableau in which pure souls can contemplate eternity. Because of the light he has spread, humanity can see things as they really are. His precious words are as sweet as new melodies. In his presence, secrets are made known and our confused thoughts come into focus. Mist is lifted from the eyes of those who consider him, and rust is dissolved from their souls. He brings news of the ancient beginning and the ultimate end; he brings meaning to every ambiguity. In the presence of such teaching, all existence becomes a poem that we recite to the rhythm of eternity.

Our knowledge is but a drop in the ocean of his knowledge; our wisdom is like a small current in the cascade of his wisdom. Measured against the seconds of his life, all of time is like an instant. Our globe, so minuscule in the scope of the universe, now rivals the vast expanses of the creation in significance, for this was the place of his birth. He is the first of *ta'ayyun*, the primordial program of the divine destiny. He is the orator of the last Prophetic word. He is the true expositor of *zahir*, and he articulates the mysteries of *batin*.[97] On the one hand, he is a sultan on the throne of Prophethood, his conscience and intellect ready to receive truths from *Ruh al-quds*,[98] and his heart sensitive to the spiritual dimensions of the universe. On the other hand, he is the most eloquent interpreter of the revelation, able to transmit whatever he receives from God to the souls and minds of others without distortion.

He teaches us about God; this is the nature of his Prophethood. He introduces us to the divine attributes and names, and such intimate knowledge stimulates in us a sense of our responsibility to God. In this respect, he is a master teacher who makes known the unknowable and helps us understand the incomprehensible. He announces

---

[97] In Islamic terminology, particularly in Sufism, *zahir* (apparent) denotes the observable dimensions of existence and the literal meaning of the Qur'an, whereas *batin* (hidden) signifies the non-observable and subtle dimensions of existence and the implicit meaning of the Qur'an.

[98] A Qur'anic term, *Ruh al-quds* (the holy or pure spirit) denotes the divine spirit that is specifically related to divine revelation and represented by the Angel Gabriel. (*See* Qur'an, 5:110; 16:102)

religious rules, preaches human virtues, and describes moral principles. He speaks with the authority of God on religious and moral questions; he is a lawmaker and the embodied explanation for the truth of truths.

Prophets and Messengers, as well as all eminent friends of God who follow them, can approach metaphysical realities, while remaining rooted in the physical realm.[99] In this lofty activity, their intellect waits upon divine revelation and is bathed in its color. Any mind that recognizes its limits and enters into this divine tutelage will be illuminated by *al-Ruh al-a'zam* and become a benefit to humanity.[100] In time, this mind will start to perceive the hidden together with the apparent, the first alongside the last.

Existence has both apparent and hidden aspects. What is apparent is seen with eyes, perceived with the senses, and understood according to reason. As for the hidden, it is a realm beyond appearance that God reveals to those whom He creates to perceive it. Prophets and Messengers perceive this hidden reality throughout their life and determine their attitudes accordingly. The master of humankind, may God's greetings be upon him, is absolutely superior in this respect; his special capacity is well-matched to his position. With the help of providence, he hears the unheard and sees the unseen. His soul transcends time and space until he surpasses even the angels and reaches the horizon of "*qab qawsayn aw adna*," the highest point of closeness to the sublime presence of God.[101]

---

[99] Muslim theologians generally differentiate between a *nabi* (Prophet) and a *rasul* (Messenger): The former is the general title for any apostles of God, whereas the latter denotes the Prophets who receive a scripture or establish a new divine law. On the other hand, *wali*, which we have translated in this edition as "eminent friend of God," denotes a perfect believer who follows the path of a Prophet or a Messenger.

[100] A Sufi concept based on Qur'anic references (70:4; 97:4), *al-Ruh al-a'zam* (the greatest spirit) is defined in several ways. In this context, it is a synonym of *Ruh al-quds* mentioned above.

[101] This idiomatic Arabic phrase means "to get so close to each other." Mentioned in the Qur'an (53:9) to describe the Prophet's early experience of divine revelation, it is interpreted in Sufi tradition as an image that signifies the highest point the Prophet, peace and blessings be upon him, reached in his heavenly journey toward the supreme presence of God.

His honored place in the sight of God is matched only by the unshakable esteem among people. Not once in his life did he abandon the truth; therefore, both his friends and enemies came to trust him. He brought the messages of God to many, preserving them in their divine beauty. He is remembered for his innocence and known for his purity. He interpreted the reality of this world and the next with a keen intelligence and enlightened soul, and he was perfectly receptive to both physical and metaphysical realms. Therefore, whoever is unprejudiced will run to him without hesitation. Even the most obdurate souls have submitted to him, and exceptional thinkers have surrendered to his wisdom.

Thanks to him, humanity transcends its corporeal nature and turns toward the spiritual life of the heart. According to the primordial divine destiny, he is the mysterious key that will unlock creation. He is the fulfillment of creation's purpose, the guide along God's straight path, and an intercessor for our eternal happiness. Before him, Prophets could only foretell what he would later say; after him, all God's eminent friends confirmed his teachings and professed that he was the cause of their attainments. Indeed, when he proclaimed "God" and brought attention to the divine unity, his proclamation had been foreshadowed by all Prophets and Messengers and would be confirmed by the spiritual discoveries of the eminent friends of God.

He was a monument of faith who lived strictly and carefully practiced what he taught. He always behaved in accordance with the world to come and lived in a deep awareness of God's presence. He was more concerned and sensitive than anyone around him and deeply aware of his responsibility. Always in pursuit of a beautiful end, he embraced his lofty task, never taking his eyes off his goal for a single moment, and he offered the treasures of his deep relationship with God to everyone.

It is he who explains the meaning of existence and relates it to its true Creator. It is he who reveals the wisdom that undergirds phenomena. He constantly reminds us that we are not alone and makes our souls feel known. Thus, he brings relief to our hearts and removes our desolation; we taste the pleasures of being at home in the world. Indeed, if we can live in the universe as in a warm house, if our hearts pulse with the love of truth, if we understand the nature of reality, it is because of the torch his words have lit in our minds. Our knowledge of existence is nothing but the unfolding of his inspiration in our souls.

He has renewed humanity in the past, is doing so in the present, and will continue to do so in the future. By his coming, he made the corrupt understandings and inhuman behaviors of his time obsolete. We believe that he will likewise cause the people of our time to hear his voice, thus proving the power of his message. People will be able to understand and interpret the truth of humanity, divinity, and the universe once again. As human beings, we will resume our dignified place within creation.

The master of humankind, may endless peace and blessings be upon him, came with a message that concerns everyone and relates to everything. People everywhere were attracted to the profundity of his mission. His temperament was distinguished by utmost perfection, his behavior by exceptional trust, and his attitudes by his constant interaction with the Divine. He enjoyed an extraordinary morality, called "*a great character*" in the Qur'an, which has never been granted to anybody else.[102] No one who even once entered his presence without prejudice could escape his influence. His beauty and superiority were augmented by the most charming speech: When he spoke, even the most eloquent wordsmiths lost their tongues and contemplated his language in silence.

God granted him depth in both his inner and outer stature. He was awe-inspiring, yet humble. Even the most arrogant souls trembled in the presence of his majesty. The haughty envoys of the Sassanid emperor stood transfixed by his grandeur and forgot what they had to say. But this gravitas was accompanied by such mildness that everyone who knew him felt as if he were part of their family and never wished to leave his presence. He stood always before the Lord, and this reality permeated his words, actions, and gestures. He inspired confidence in everyone, he was always trustworthy, and in his presence, only songs of confidence could be heard.

---

[102] Qur'an, 68:4.

His behavior brought reason and spirit, logic and feeling, into equilibrium. He was renowned for his intelligence, his insight that never misled, and his resoluteness that allowed no hesitation. His work and perseverance, his strategic decisions, his refusal to surrender to even the most formidable obstacles, his laughter in the face of adversity, his ability to find meaning in hardship, his perfect composure in the midst of struggle: all were outstanding. By his bravery, he transformed defeats into victories and fashioned achievements out of apparent failures.

As a family leader, he was peerless. He was a perfect mentor to his friends and knew how to win hearts with his mild manners. He was a matchless guide, never misleading his followers. He was a master of speech, a godly man of the heart, a sage, a chief of state, and a victorious commander. Despite being the peak of perfection, he always considered himself just one man among many. He did not wish to be praised or honored as he surely deserved, and he advised his friends not to show him excessive respect.

He was the origin and final cause of creation, but he did not consider himself with undue importance. Although he was the greatest sultan of the spiritual realm, he lived exceptionally modestly, as if maintaining a lifelong fast. Instead of eating, he fed others; instead of adorning himself, he clothed others. He always acted out of a deep gratitude, giving thanks to God a hundred times for even the smallest blessing. He surpassed the angels in his knowledge, love, and awe of God. He was in the world but was not worldly. He was traveling toward another world, but for the sake of God alone, not in order to receive any reward. His heart was with his Lord, and his eyes were fixed on the works that manifest His names. For him, this world was an inlet in the ocean of the next, or a field of cultivation that would be harvested in the Hereafter. Thus, he dedicated all his exceptional efforts to the life to come. He was as generous as the wind, which carries seeds across the world and leaves them there to grow. He looked after the poor and fed the hungry, often going hungry himself. When he died, he had no palace or estate, no wealth or riches. Nor could he leave possessions to his family. He lived in the world humbly and left it humbly. Surely, he did not abandon the world, just as he never indulged it. Instead, he judged this life according to its true worth, and regarded the next world according to its infinite value.

Despite his dignity, nobility, and relationship with God, he was so humble that newcomers would barely notice him. It was as if he held these two opposites together. Ignoring any reverence shown to him by his friends, he continued to share the ground with them, share his meals with them, and disguise his uniqueness as if it was a great secret. He joked with those around him to make them feel comfortable. He ornamented his dignity with humility, balanced his majesty with compassion, and always privileged his humanity over the eminence of his task.

He was moderate, calm, and balanced at all times. He acted gently, even in the face of great affliction. He knew how to calm the rage and fury of those around him and how to soften the fiercest enemies with a single word. When he was forced into combat, he quickly sought mediation. As long as the rights of people were not violated, he would treat his aggressors with forgiveness and tolerance, as the historical literature on his life abundantly demonstrates. His trustworthiness was without precedent. He never broke his promise or went back on his word, neither before his Prophethood nor after. He lived as a monument of fidelity, never speaking falsely or even alluding to untruth.

He did not hold a pen, was never introduced to a book, and had no teacher. This was to ensure his perfection as the universal teacher. This way, his interpretation of the divine commandments would not be adulterated by any foreign knowledge. In other words, God protected His own commandments by keeping His Messenger free from external influences. Only in this sense was he unlettered. But as the universal teacher, his words have astonished the most erudite scholars and the most eminent geniuses, the most sophisticated minds and the most enlightened souls. Indeed, history testifies to the power of his speech, the soundness of his judgment, and the perfection of his work.

He presented an abundant treasure of knowledge. The news he brought concerning the distant past faced no objection, and the statements he made concerning the religion and culture of prehistoric nations were never challenged. This is natural, for it was God who gave this information to His Messenger. He was a sultan of speech, a monument of reason, and a vast ocean of thought, as immense as his mission. His expressions were so fluent, his statements so clear, and his style so rich that he could reveal a world of truth to his audience with a mere sentence or two. Sometimes he spoke volumes of wisdom in a single word, volumes that he entrusted to the interpretation of later masters of exegesis. "I have been given comprehensive words," he said, referring to this divine blessing in him.

He would be asked hundreds of questions at once and would respond to all of them without hesitation. He addressed the people in a style they could understand. He avoided confusion and clarified his intentions with succinct expressions so that all could benefit from his teachings and be satisfied, whether learned or ignorant, young or old. He delivered many sermons, addressed various concerns, analyzed different subjects, and always spoke the truth. Even his fiercest enemies never accused him of a single lie.

It would be unfair or even irrational to assume that such a man, who spent two-thirds of his life fortified against even the least untruth, might proclaim the divine revelation falsely. His words and judgments encompassed the past, present, and future. He spoke of faith, set rules regarding worship, and made pronouncements on social, economic, military, and administrative topics. He practiced what he taught and harvested the fruits of his practice. History has certified the truth of his proclamations, and thousands of commentators, philosophers, and scholars after him have acknowledged the wisdom of his words. Millions of eminent friends of God have embraced his guidance, affirming each of his judgments. Truly he stands unique among human history; his magnificent legacy of knowledge and wisdom encompassing all aspects of existence.

January 2003

Sources

HUMANITY & CIVILIZATION

The Love of Humanity
"İnsanı Sevmek" *Sızıntı*, September 1999, Issue 248.
The Inner Life of Humanity
"İç Derinlikleriyle İnsan" *Sızıntı*, August 1999, Issue 247.
Our Own Depths (I)
"Kendi Derinlikleriyle İnsan - I" *Sızıntı*, May 1993, Issue 172.
Our Own Depths (II)
"Kendi Derinlikleriyle İnsan - II" *Sızıntı*, June 1993, Sayı 173.
Our Responsibility
"Yeri ve Sorumluluklarıyla İnsan" *Sızıntı*, April 1999, Issue 243.
Woman from a Spiritual Point of View
"Dar Bir Çerçevede Kadın" *Yağmur*, April 2000, Issue 7.
The Society of Peace
"Huzur Topluluğu" *Sızıntı*, August 1979, Issue 7.
The Ideal Society
"İdeal Cemiyet" *Sızıntı*, June 1990, Issue 137.
The Concept of Civilization
"Medeniyet ve Mefhum Kargaşası" *Sızıntı*, August 1985, Issue 79.
The Nature We Have Destroyed
"Tahrip Edilen Tabiat" *Sızıntı*, January 1990, Issue 132.
Toward the Sovereignty of the Heart
"Kalplerin Sultanlığına Doğru" *Sızıntı*, August 1995, Issue 199.
Humanity Longing for Love
"İnsanlık Sevgiye Hasret Gidiyor" *Sızıntı*, March 2008, Issue 350.

FAITH & WISDOM

The Love of God
"Allah Sevgisi" *Sızıntı*, June and July 2003, Issues 293 and 294.

The Believer Standing before God
"Allah Karşısındaki Duruşuyla Mümin" *Sızıntı*, May 2006, Issue 328.
The Characteristics of a Believer
"İnanmış İnsanın Nitelikleri" *Sızıntı*, May 1999, Issue 244.
The Purpose of Life
"Hayatın Gayesi" *Sızıntı*, July 1997, Issue 222.
The Love of Truth
"Hakikat Aşkı" *Sızıntı*, May 2004, Issue 304.

MORALS & SPIRITUALITY

The Heart
"Gönül" *Sızıntı*, August 1990, Issue 139.
Love
"Sevgi" *Sızıntı*, March 1987, Issue 98.
Mercy
"Merhamet" *Sızıntı*, November 1980, Issue 22.
Forgiveness and Tolerance
"Müsamaha" *Sızıntı*, March 1980, Issue 14.
Virtue and Happiness
"Fazilet ve Mutluluk" *Sızıntı*, June 1982, Issue 41.
Inner Peace
"Huzur Ufku" *Sızıntı*, Fabruary 2000, Issue 253.
A Portrait of the Man of the Heart
"Bir Gönül İnsanı Portresi" *Sızıntı*, August 2000, Issue 259.

EDUCATION

The Youth
"Gençlik" *Zuhur*, August 1977, Issue 3.
Elevating Humanity
"İnsanı Yükseltme" *Sızıntı*, July 1979, Issue 6.
Our Philosophy of Education (I)
"Bizim Maarifimiz - I" *Sızıntı*, October 1979, Issue 9.
Our Philosophy of Education (II)
"Bizim Maarifimiz - II" *Sızıntı*, November 1979, Issue 10.
What Education Promises
"Maarifin Vaad Ettikleri" *Sızıntı*, March 1984, Issue 62.

What to Expect from Education
"Nesillerin Maariften Bekledikleri" *Sızıntı*, April 1984, Issue 63.

PEOPLE OF SERVICE

The People We are Longing For
"Hasretini Çektiğimiz İnsan" *Sızıntı*, February 1980, Issue 13.
The Architects of Our Future
"Geleceğin Mimarları" *Sızıntı*, September 1980, Issue 20.
The New Man
"Yeni İnsan" *Sızıntı*, March 1991, Issue 146.
Devout Architects of the Soul
"Ruh Mimarları Rabbanîler" *Yeni Ümit*, April 1995, Issue 28.
The Souls Devoted to God
"Hakk'a Adanmış Ruhlar" *Sızıntı*, October 2000, Issue 261.

ISLAM

The Nature of Islamic Religion
"Din Ufku" *Sızıntı*, November 1997, Issue 226.
Resting in the Shade of Islam
"İslam'ın Gölgesinde Hayat" *Sızıntı*, November 2000, Issue 262.
Characteristics of Islam
"İslam Düşüncesinin Ana Karakteristiği" *Yeni Ümit*, April 1999, Issue 44.
A Partial Description of Our System of Thought
"Dar Bir Zaviyeden Düşünce Sistemimiz" *Yeni Ümit*, July 2000, Issue 49.
The Last Messenger of the Unseen
"Ve Gaybın Son Habercisi" *Yeni Ümit*, January 2003, Issue 59.

INDEX

Q

R

religion, x, xi, xii, 18, 37, 44, 54, 106, 146, 155, 156, 157, 158, 159, 165, 169, 183

religious traditions, xi, 44, 169

renaissance, ix, 139

research, 77, 122, 157

respect, x, xi, xiii, 5, 8, 20, 21, 25, 26, 27, 28, 29, 33, 45, 53, 55, 61, 64, 83, 93, 96, 102, 118, 140, 170, 178, 179, 182

responsibility, ix, x, 20, 21, 31, 36, 72, 88, 100, 115, 125, 127, 130, 133, 140, 141, 143, 145, 146, 161, 168, 171, 176, 178, 180

resurrection, ix, 100

reunion, 60, 69, 83, 157

revelation, xii, 20, 156, 158, 162, 173, 174, 176, 178, 179, 184

revival, ix, xii, 164, 174

reward, 22, 32, 105, 149, 152, 182

rights, 25, 26, 28, 89, 104, 158, 183

Roman Empire, 127

Roman revolution, 109

Rome, 9

rote learning, 118, 122

Rumi, viii, ix, 5, 10, 21, 49, 136

S

Said ibn Jubayr, 157

salvation, 143

sanctuary, 88, 92, 100, 117

Sarakhsi, 158

Sassanid emperor, 181

satisfaction, 17, 31, 32, 60, 159, 163

school, 4, 117, 118, 122, 123, 155

science, viii, 18, 36, 45, 113, 114, 140, 146, 150, 155, 156, 169, 177

scientific achievements, 103

scientific research, 77

second nature, 10, 47, 110, 168

security, 28, 46, 99, 101, 126, 145, 163, 170

seeds of goodness, x, xi, 114

self, 13, 15, 28, 35, 45, 46, 55, 59, 64, 71, 83, 87, 114, 117, 139, 157, 175

self-annihilation, 45, 59

self-awareness, 13

self-consciousness, 13

self-control, 13, 71

self-criticism, 46

self-discipline, 64, 175

self-interrogation, 157

self-knowledge, 13

self-renewal, 35

separation, 20, 53, 60, 69, 169

serenity, 27, 77

servants, xii, 22, 33, 46, 57, 60, 86

service, vii, viii, x, 8, 20, 21, 22, 32, 33, 35, 46, 54, 57, 58, 59, 63, 64, 101, 104, 105, 106, 125, 126, 129, 135, 140, 143, 147, 149, 151, 158, 163, 167, 168, 177

service to God, 22, 63, 140, 158, 177

service to humanity, 63, 106

shared conscience, 144, 158

sincerity, xiii, 23, 68, 105, 144, 151, 171

social harmony, 170

social life, 21, 167

social order, x, 20, 26

social relations, 167, 171

social services, 140

society, ix, x, xiii, 3, 9, 15, 17, 27, 28, 29, 31, 32, 33, 35, 36, 37, 43, 44, 67, 88, 93, 102, 103, 126, 129, 133, 134, 140, 143, 145, 149, 150, 156, 157, 163, 167, 171

Socrates, 13, 95

solidarity, 28, 104

universal responsibility, 143

universe, 4, 5, 7, 8, 19, 20, 24, 31, 49, 55, 61, 67, 68, 69, 71, 72, 75, 76, 85, 87, 88, 96, 101, 103, 110, 121, 130, 133, 134, 135, 141, 144, 155, 157, 162, 164, 165, 169, 172, 173, 177, 178, 180, 181

V

vicegerency, 19, 20, 21, 101

vicegerent, 19, 22, 162, 163

violence, 33, 134

virtue, vii, ix, x, xi, 9, 10, 18, 28, 29, 35, 43, 44, 68, 86, 91, 92, 93, 95, 96, 97, 99, 102, 114, 117, 118, 123, 125, 130, 149, 168, 172

vision, viii, xii, 18, 36, 103, 134, 139, 155

W

war, 48, 53, 70

water of life, 89, 133

way of life, 140, 169

weakness, 61, 70, 156, 175

wealth, 43, 45, 54, 66, 96, 130, 136, 145, 149, 182

West, vii, 169

Western philosophy, viii, 170

willpower, 14, 19, 27, 31, 64, 72, 99, 127

wisdom, x, xi, 5, 7, 8, 10, 13, 19, 31, 32, 37, 43, 44, 45, 60, 65, 67, 69, 71, 72, 77, 83, 95, 100, 114, 117, 118, 122, 133, 134, 140, 141, 158, 161, 167, 168, 176, 178, 180, 184

worldliness, 150

worship, 20, 21, 26, 46, 54, 57, 58, 68, 75, 156, 167, 168, 171, 172, 184

Y

young generation, 109, 110

youth, viii, 6, 25, 57, 73, 109, 110, 111, 122, 123, 125, 130

Yunus, 49, 135